ALL-TIME FAVORITE

SHEET CAKES & SLAB PIES

ALL-TIME FAVORITE

SHEET CAKES & SLAB PIES

Easy to Make, Easy to Serve

BRUCE WEINSTEIN *and*
MARK SCARBROUGH

Photographs by ERIC MEDSKER

St. Martin's Griffin
New York

www.stmartins.com

Book design by Susan Walsh

The Library of Congress Cataloging-in-Publication Data is available upon request.

ISBN 978-1-250-11758-8 (trade paperback)
ISBN 978-1-250-11759-5 (e-book)

Our books may be purchased in bulk for promotional, educational, or business use. Please contact your local bookseller or the Macmillan Corporate and Premium Sales Department at 1-800-221-7945, extension 5442, or by email at MacmillanSpecialMarkets@macmillan.com.

First Edition: October 2017

10 9 8 7 6 5 4 3 2

ALSO BY BRUCE WEINSTEIN
AND MARK SCARBROUGH

À la Mode

*Turbo Blender
Dessert Revolution*

CONTENTS

Coffee Cakes & Cheesecakes

Classic Slab Pies

Chocolate Slab Pies & Other Favorites

Sheet Strudel, Danish, Shortbread & More

INTRODUCTION

Picture this: It's a summer afternoon, probably a weekend, maybe even a holiday. You got up early to pack the car and drive to a picnic shelter you rented months ago. Maybe it's by a lake, the soft plash of people swimming nearby. Or maybe it's near a cool stream, its rhythmic burble a counterpoint to the Spotify list you've got going as you unload. A slight breeze softens the morning thrum of the sun. The sky promises an arching, aching blue all afternoon.

You've been looking forward to this family reunion for a long time. Or maybe it's a company picnic. Or a church potluck. Or a retirement party. Or just a get-together with friends. Anyway, there's going to be fried chicken. You made sure of that. Several are bringing salads and slaws. There'll be platters of deli slices, bread for sandwiches, and pickles galore. Cars pull up. People shake hands, maybe formal at first, and then they give in and go for bear hugs. As the kids head for the water, you pull out a big metal sheet pan filled rim to rim with a cake or a pie. Everybody smiles. It's going to be a great day.

We're all about these big all-American single-layer desserts made in a sheet pan. They've got a frosting-to-cake or a fruit-to-crust ratio that'll satisfy just about everyone.

They're brazen abundance. So if you're going to a family reunion or a potluck, or if you've got a birthday party or a barbecue coming up, or if you've got a lot of people coming over, or if you eat cake for the frosting and pie for the filling, or if you hanker for the days when people made sheet cakes and slab pies for no other reason than that they were the easiest way to make a big dessert without a lot of fuss, put on your eating pants and get busy.

A Sheet Cake versus a Slab Pie

A sheet cake is a large rectangular cake—not a layer cake, but rather a big slab that fills a lipped sheet pan. As far as we're concerned, it's *not* made in a 9 x 13-inch baking pan. Mind you, there's nothing wrong with a single-layer 9 x 13-inch cake. It's just a bit too much like a casserole for our purposes. (More on the precise equipment in a bit.)

A true sheet cake is not very tall, maybe only an inch or so high—which means you never have to apportion frosting bite for bite in a serving. In fact, a sheet cake by our definition has frosting just about equal in depth to the cake itself. And if there's no frosting, there'd better be a lot of whipped cream or a rich glaze.

Made in the same exact pan, a slab pie has a crust (sometimes graham cracker, sometimes pastry) under a fruit or cream filling that's thinner than a traditional pie, more jam-like, too, if it's a fruit pie, or a little more firmly set if it's a custard pie. Yes, there are double-crust slab pies among our recipes. More often, there's a bottom crust, a rich filling, and then a crumble or even a meringue topping.

We also have recipes here for specialty items like sheet coffee cakes and cheesecakes. We pull out the stops for slab Danishes and some retro desserts like Midwestern Slab Pudding. And there's even one fancy, traditional Greek tart with a custard layer between sheets of crisp phyllo. But these are curiosities. Our main focus is on cake and pie.

Getting the Right Pan

Every recipe in this book is made in a *13 x 18-inch sheet pan with a 1- to 1½-inch lipped edge.* In industry lingo, it's called "a half-size sheet pan" or sometimes just a "half-sheet"—meaning it's half the size of a standard restaurant-service sheet pan (which won't fit in most home ovens).

Get a ruler. Measure. Be precise. We're not talking about a cookie sheet, which has at most two lipped edges (or sometimes none). We're also not talking about an 11 x 17-inch sheet pan called a "baking sheet" in American cookery. And we're certainly not talking about a 10 x 15-inch jelly-roll pan. None of these will work, although we will get to a few solutions in a bit.

Still, we can think of two scenarios when even the right pan won't work. First, if you've got an insulated sheet pan, some of these batters won't set in the time we state. Or you'll end up with gooey centers and soggy crusts with some slab pies. We've calibrated the recipes to work with a noninsulated metal surface, the better to catch and hold lots of heat.

And second, if your half-sheet is beaten up, warped, or as buckled as the bumper of an unrefurbished '76 Ford Pinto, you're setting yourself up for endless frustration. The thing won't sit flat on an oven rack. It won't bake an even cake or pie. So toss it out and buy a new half-sheet. A very nice one runs about twenty bucks.

Prepping the Half-Sheet Pan

Once you've got the right pan, you may need to grease and flour it before you can make a cake or a pie. Here are the rules. First, use whatever fat the cake or pie crust requires: butter, shortening, walnut oil, vegetable oil, etc. If it's butter or shortening and thus solid at room temperature, put a little glob on a piece of wax paper or on a paper towel and run the fat all over the inside of the pan. If the cake or pie crust recipe calls for oil, pour some onto a paper towel and do the same operation. Don't scrimp. With a few rare, marked exceptions, be generous. And get obsessive. Smear every corner, the whole interior surface, and even up the sides. Remember: these are large-format pans. *It can take up to half a stick of butter to grease the inside of one properly.*

Second, if you also have to flour the pan, once again be generous. Dump in plenty of flour—say, ¼ cup—and tilt the pan this way and that *over the sink* until the pan's interior bottom and sides are evenly coated in a fine, white film. Tap the corners on your counter to get the flour moving. You'll also see any spots you missed when you were greasing the thing. Fix these and let the excess flour skim across them for a light, even coating.

At the end of the whole process, tap any excess flour into the garbage can.

Of course, there's an easier way: nonstick spray. Apply an oil-based spray for a pan that only needs to be greased or a fat-and-flour spray (usually called a "baking spray") for a pan that needs to be both buttered (or oiled) and floured. To be blunt, one of us (the chef—his name's first in our team) prefers the spraying method, even if the fats don't match up, even if it's a buttery cake and an oil-based spray. He's spent too much time in the kitchen. The other of us, the writer (aka the idealist) prefers the original, old-school method without aerosol shenanigans. Follow your heart, but avoid the fakery of butter-flavored sprays.

Solutions for Other Types of Pans

What if you don't have a half-sheet pan? If you've got an 11 x 17-inch lipped sheet pan, you can indeed make these recipes, but you'll have to lose about 20 percent of what you make. Make the batter, crust, filling, or frosting as directed, then take about a fifth away, either discarding it or baking it in a small baking vessel, perhaps several indentations of a muffin tin or small ramekins. The remnants won't be perfect but they won't be wasted.

However, if you've got a 10 x 15-inch

jelly-roll pan, you're in better luck. For sheet cakes and coffee cakes, weigh the batter (if possible) by setting a clean bowl onto a kitchen scale, using the tare feature to zero out the weight, and then scraping the prepared batter into that bowl. Figure out two-thirds of the total weight. Pour this amount into a jelly-roll pan (greased and floured as the recipe requires). You'll need to set the prepared jelly-roll pan on the scale, zero out the weight, and add batter until you've reached two-thirds of the total weight. Now put the remaining batter into a 9-inch square baking pan (greased and floured as required). Yes, you can eyeball this whole operation but taking the weight will give you a far more accurate marker for the two pans.

For slab pies and cheesecakes, make the crust as directed, then use two-thirds of the mixture for the jelly-roll pan and the rest for a 9-inch square baking pan (pressing or rolling it out as necessary). Eyeball this step but be more accurate with the filling, weighing it out and doing your calculations to get two-thirds of it into the jelly-roll pan.

As to baking the (now two) sheet cakes or coffeecakes, set the oven timer for half the stated time in the recipe. Neither pan's cake or pie will be ready. However, you'll see how the cake is setting. As you see the top dry out and firm up, start testing with a toothpick or a cake tester to hit the desired degree of doneness (a few moist crumbs attached, the toothpick dry, or other visual cues). In general, the 9-inch square cake will be done before the jelly-roll cake (although thicker batters can take the same timing in each).

And as to baking the (now two) slab pies or cheesecakes, again start checking at that halfway point. In this case, however, the jelly-roll cake may well finish before the 9-inch one, particularly with fruit pies, mostly because of the difference in the heights of the sides of the two pans.

And one more thing: once you get the cakes or pies out of the oven, make sure you note your new timings in the margin of the recipe in this book.

About Serving Sizes

We haven't included serving sizes or yields. Everything is made in the same size pan, so everything serves about the same number. Our best guess is that each big sheet cake or slab pie makes between sixteen and twenty-four servings. But we once sent *seven* of these cakes and pies to a beach weekend that included twelve adults and five teenagers. After forty-eight hours, we were told there was one lone piece left!

Yes, these are made for crowds. Honestly, that's about the only reason most of us bake anymore. Gone are the days when people would throw together a pie for a Wednesday night. We break out the stand mixer for a rabble. We should relish the abundance.

Using an Offset Spatula

These batters can be thick. The frostings, too. They need to be spread, so you'll need an offset spatula, a long, thin, narrow metal blade with an oval end and a crook near the handle so the blade "steps down" about an inch or so.

That bend allows you to distribute pressure evenly along the metal surface, thereby applying a more constant force to spread out thick batters and gooey frostings. Move the spatula in wide swaths, this way and that, pressing down gently but deliberately and thereby creating an even layer of whatever you've got underneath. You'll need this tool to spread many of the very thick batters in these recipes as well as the icings and frostings that go on top of the sheet cakes.

Frankly, an offset spatula is the best investment for these recipes. It's sometimes called an "angled icing spatula," an "offset icing spatula," or a "cake knife scraper spatula." No matter, you can find it at cookware stores and online outlets.

Seven Recipe Standards Throughout This Book

1. Avoid substitutions.

We actually had this conversation once:

"Your recipes don't work!"
"What did you do?"
"I just substituted cornstarch for the flour."
"What?"
"Well, they're both white."

Listen, cooking is physics, the thunder and lightning of heat and sizzle. Baking, our concern here, is chemistry, a fussy set of ratios and equivalents. If you don't stick closely to the stated ingredients and their amounts, your dessert can end up a mess. A word to the wise should be sufficient.

2. Heat the oven to the stated temperature.

Don't cheat. If your oven takes fifteen minutes to get to 350°F, let it have the full time.

3. Use room-temperature eggs.

The proteins should be loosened up and ready for a good workout in order to beat the most air into the batter for the best loft and structure. To get the eggs to room temperature, either leave them in their shells on the counter for 20 minutes or crack them into a small bowl and set them aside at room temperature for 10 minutes.

4. But use cold butter in the batters.

Again, it's all about air. You want to beat in the most possible for a tender crumb. Luscious, spreadable, room-temperature butter is too loosey-goosey to hold air well. So the butter needs to be somewhere around 50°F. Take it out of your 40°F fridge and cut it into small chunks. Put these in the mixing bowl and gather your other ingredients. By the time you're good to go, the butter won't be frigid but it will still be cool and firm. It can now trap air.

That said, you'll need room-temperature, softened butter for many of the frostings and buttercreams. Read the recipe carefully to know what you need to have in hand.

5. Scrape down the inside of the bowl several times.

As you're beating the butter, eggs, and/ or sugar with an electric mixer, occasionally turn off the machine and scrape down the inside of the bowl with a silicone spatula. You need to get any undissolved or unincorporated bits even throughout so they can be readily incorporated. Don't miss the bottom of the bowl, where butter and shortening tend to clump. A uniform batter is a successful batter. You can hardly overdo this scraping down.

6. Add the eggs to the batter one at a time unless otherwise indicated.

You want to get their long-chain proteins distributed into the fat without swamping the batter.

7. Only use low-fat or fat-free products when the recipe says you can.

Assume that every dairy product is "full fat." We'll let you know when low-fat or even fat-free ingredients offer the same results.

A Couple of Notes About Flour

These recipes—except for the gluten-free ones—use either cake flour or all-purpose flour. Cake flour is a low-protein (low-gluten) flour that *can* give a better crumb and loft to each slice. All-purpose flour has a higher gluten signature and *can* give a better density and chew to each slice. The only hesitation (the "can" in those sentences) has to do with the amount of beating the flour endures and its ratio to the sugars and fats in the mix.

We have chosen the best flour for each recipe. As a general rule, do not substitute cake flour for all-purpose flour. However, in an emergency you can substitute all-purpose flour for cake flour. Use 15 tablespoons of all-purpose flour plus 1 tablespoon of cornstarch for every 1 cup (that is, 16 tablespoons) of cake flour. In other words, reduce the flour by 1 tablespoon per cup and then make up the difference with cornstarch. The results will not be as perfect—the cake can cook a little faster and brown a little too deeply—but you still will get the job done in a reasonable fashion.

And one more thing: as Alice Medrich has taught us, every baking book should reveal the way its authors measure flour. As far as we're concerned, dip and overfill the measuring cup in the bag or canister. Do not compress the flour into the cup against the sides of the bag or canister. Instead, lift the cup out and scrape off the excess with a flatware knife, leveling the cup so there are no indentations.

Four Other Common Ingredients

We use these a lot, so a word or two about them might be helpful.

1. Buttermilk

There are two kinds sold in our supermarkets: the now-standard, *cultured* sort that is like wet yogurt; and the more traditional, old-school buttermilk that's the leavings from making butter. This second, artisanal type is available at high-end or large supermarkets. It's thinner, definitely more watery. It's not the best here. We have used only the former, cultured buttermilk, in testing these recipes.

2. Peanut butter

There are two styles of peanut butter: natural and standard. Natural-style peanut butter does not have any added fat or sugar; it's just ground peanuts, often with salt. The oil usually separates. Stir it back into the jar before using. So-called "standard-style" peanut butter has added fat and sometimes added sugar as well as salt. The oil never separates. Do not confuse these two types in these recipes. If we've called for natural-style, we don't want any added fat (or sugar). If we've called for standard-style, we're relying on that extra bump of fat to make a cake tender or a frosting silky. These two styles are then divided the two types we all know: creamy (or smooth) and crunchy (or chunky). We'll indicate exactly which one we mean in each recipe.

3. Solid vegetable shortening

We grew up with Crisco or Spry, the twentieth-century standards when it comes to shortening. These will definitely work here. However, we can now find non-hydrogenated shortening in most supermarkets. It's not firm at room temperature, so it needs to be stored in the refrigerator and used like butter, cold and firm. We do not recommend using margarine or butter-flavored shortening sticks.

4. Unsalted butter

Why would you let someone else control the salt content of your baked goods? And why would you let them do so with what's often third-rate salt? Unsalted butter is the baking standard. Millions of pastry chefs can't be wrong.

Two Visual Cues

We use these cookery shorthands again and again. Here's what we mean.

1. Beat the eggs and sugar until you can make wide ribbons.

In other words, beat the mixture until it thickens a bit—and then take it further, until it's almost fluffy. When you dip the turned-off beaters into the mixture, you should be able to lift them up and see wide, smooth ribbons (rather than dribbles and thin streams) fall back onto the batter below. Those ribbons will lie on top of the batter without immediately dissolving (although they will eventually do so).

2. Beat the egg whites or heavy cream until you can make soft or firm peaks.

This is all about how much air you can get into either ingredient. At soft peaks, you can dip the turned-off beaters into the mass and form droopy, saggy cones off the beaters' edges as you turn them this way and that. At firm peaks, the little cones will hold themselves upright no matter which way you turn the beaters. But be careful: you can indeed beat in too much air. Either the egg whites will break into a foamy watery mixture or the cream will churn to something like very soft butter.

And One More Thing . . .

Don't be scared of excess. Throw a party. Get the neighbors. Call your family. Facebook a meet-up. Make it happen. You've got enough cake or pie. Don't look back. Have a great time. As we crafted this book, we sure did.

CLASSIC SHEET CAKES

Mostly Chocolate

A lot of people know about the Texas sheet cake: a chocolate cake, usually with a fudgy frosting, sometimes studded with pecans. It's terrific, no doubt. But there's so much more! Here are our chocolate concoctions to match that popular favorite as well as lots of classics like rich vanilla cakes, buttermilk cakes, and even a few surprises like a sheet cake version of jam thumbprint cookies.

The Crumb

It means the way the cake's structure manifests, not on the plate, but on the fork. It means the cake breaks into tidbits, like airy morsels. They should be neither so damp that they glom together nor so dry that they shard apart. They should be moist enough to have some give when gently pressed (the crumb's "elasticity"). With the exceptions of sponge cakes and a few cookie-cake hybrids, a particularly satisfying and dense crumb only happens when you beat the various ingredients in the proper way. Here's how.

Beat the cool butter and sugar together for a long while. Only cool butter can trap enough air to build a proper structure. Take it out of the fridge, then gather the other ingredients together. By the time you're ready, it'll be about 50°F, perfect for these batters. And truth be told, you almost can't overdo beating it with the sugar. Don't walk the dog, but keep the machine running until the mixture in the bowl is luxurious, almost fluffy. You want to incorporate lots of air.

Once you add the flour, ease up considerably and beat the mixture as little as possible (unless otherwise indicated). If you stretch the glutens, you'll end up with a tough cake. Only get the flour evenly moistened and uniformly distributed; the batter may still be a tad grainy.

We sometimes call for an admittedly unusual technique. Old-school recipes often ask you to beat in the flour and a liquid (like milk) in alternating amounts—say, a third of the flour, then half the milk, then half the remaining flour, and so on. In many of our recipes, we've nixed this folderol: Turn off the mixer, pour the flour mixture evenly over what's in the bowl, then beat at *low speed* while you pour in the liquid in a slow, steady stream. We found we got airier, lighter sheet cakes with this nonstandard method.

What Goes on Top of That Crumb

Here's what's what. A glaze is a thin, often translucent syrup poured over the top of the cake. In most cases, it is not spreadable—or certainly not for very long as it begins to cool. Work quickly with the courage of your convictions.

A frosting, by contrast, is spreadable, even moundable. There's an old distinction between icings and frostings: the former are made with milk; the latter, with butter. We have simply called many of the spreadable, moundable concoctions "frostings." They are often made with cream cheese, butter, shortening, or some combination thereof.

Then there are the buttercreams. In essence, there are two types. An American buttercream is made with confectioners' sugar and butter, usually with an added flavor. It's a sturdy, fairly simple affair. We sometimes make a nonstandard variation, replacing some of the butter with cream cheese because we like the snap it brings to the dessert.

A French buttercream is a more elaborate confection: egg yolks are beaten first with a cooked sugar syrup until cool, and then with lots and lots of butter. We'll offer you tips and tricks when you get to these. They're temperamental. Take care.

Still Want a Layer Cake?

Use a 3- to 4-inch cookie or biscuit cutter to cut the cooled cake into small rounds. Or use a nonstick-safe knife to cut the cake into small squares (or even more elaborate shapes) right in the pan. Gently lift these out and stack them on top of each other, frosting a little between the layers and then all over the tops and sides to create individual three- or four-tier layer cakes.

Finally . . .

Buy a box of toothpicks. You're going to need them. Or even splurge for a metal cake tester. Timing is a mere suggestion in baking. Always go by the visual cues: a few moist crumbs on the toothpick or tester, for example. A great cake deserves the best care.

CHOCOLATE CAKE WITH
CARAMEL BUTTERCREAM AND PRETZELS

Never make our basic chocolate sheet cake when you're home alone! It's irresistible: topped with salty pretzels, laced with caramel sauce, set over a superrich buttercream made with caramel sauce, with a light, almost delicate chocolate cake underneath. It's as if a fine, fancy layer cake batter morphed into a big ol' sheet cake that will stand up to the incredible caramel/chocolate/ pretzel fandango on top.

For the cake

19 tablespoons (2 sticks plus 3 tablespoons) cool unsalted butter, cut into small chunks, plus additional for the sheet pan

2¼ cups plus 2 tablespoons all-purpose flour, plus additional for the sheet pan

6 tablespoons unsweetened cocoa powder

1 cup warm water (about 100°F)

1¼ teaspoons baking soda

½ teaspoon salt

1 cup plus 3 tablespoons granulated white sugar

1 cup plus 3 tablespoons packed light brown sugar

2 large eggs plus 1 large egg white, at room temperature

½ cup full-fat sour cream

1 tablespoon vanilla extract

1. Position the rack in the center of the oven. Heat the oven to 350°F. Generously butter and lightly flour the inside of a 13 x 18-inch lipped sheet pan.

2. Whisk the cocoa powder into the water in a small bowl until smooth. Set aside to cool for 30 minutes. Meanwhile, whisk the flour, baking soda, and salt in a medium bowl until uniform.

3. Using a handheld electric mixer or a stand mixer with the paddle attachment, beat the butter and both sugars in a large bowl at medium speed until light, velvety, and fluffy, about 5 minutes. Beat in the eggs one at a time, then beat in the egg white. Scrape down the inside of the bowl, then beat in the sour cream and vanilla until smooth and uniform.

4. With the mixer at low speed, beat in half the flour mixture. Pour in half the cocoa mixture and beat until smooth. Now beat in the remaining flour mixture, followed by the rest of the cocoa mixture. Make sure there are no dry specks of flour down at the bottom of the bowl, then use an offset spatula to spread the thick batter evenly into the prepared pan.

5. Bake until set and a toothpick or cake tester inserted into the center of the cake comes out with a few moist crumbs attached, 18 to 20 minutes. Cool in the pan on a wire rack to room temperature, about 2 hours.

For the buttercream

19 tablespoons (2 sticks plus 3 tablespoons) unsalted butter, softened to room temperature

1¼ cups jarred caramel sauce

⅓ cup full-fat sour cream
1½ teaspoons vanilla extract
2 to 3 cups confectioners' sugar
3 cups crushed salty pretzels, preferably pretzel
    nuggets, for topping

1. Using a handheld electric mixer or a stand mixer with the whisk attachment, beat the butter and ¾ cup of the caramel sauce in a clean, dry large bowl until smooth, about 2 minutes. Then beat in the sour cream and vanilla.

2. With the mixer at low speed, beat in 1 cup of the confectioners' sugar until smooth. Beat in 1 additional cup until smooth. Continue beating, adding more confectioners' sugar in ¼-cup increments, until the frosting is smooth and spreadable but thick enough to hold its shape on the side of a spatula. Using an offset spatula, spread and smooth the frosting over the cooled cake. Set aside at room temperature to firm up, about 20 minutes.

3. To serve, sprinkle the top of the cake with the crushed pretzels, then drizzle with the remaining ½ cup caramel sauce.

TESTER NOTES
Choose a jarred caramel sauce without a lot of chemical flavor enhancements. Better yet, look for a jarred butterscotch caramel sauce, like an ice cream topping.

ONE-BOWL CHOCOLATE CAKE WITH CHOCOLATE-COCONUT BUTTERCREAM

Don't let the simplicity fool you! This is one seriously moist and fudgy cake. True, there's no mixer involved, even for the frosting. But you will have to apply some elbow grease to that whisk. The frosting is a fairly standard American buttercream, just a sweetened, buttery confection, given a little grainy texture with the shredded coconut. Together, the results are dense and chewy, a great last-minute sheet cake when you don't have time for fancier fare.

For the cake
1½ cups canola or vegetable oil, plus additional
    for the sheet pan
2¼ cups granulated white sugar
3 large eggs, at room temperature
2¼ cups regular cultured buttermilk
2 teaspoons vanilla extract
½ cup unsweetened cocoa powder
1¾ cups all-purpose flour
1 cup rolled oats
2 teaspoons baking soda
½ teaspoon salt

1. Position the rack in the center of the oven. Heat the oven to 350°F. Lightly oil the inside of a 13 x 18-inch lipped sheet pan.

2. Whisk the sugar and oil in a large bowl until smooth, about 1 minute. Whisk in the eggs until well combined, then whisk in the buttermilk and vanilla.

3. Whisk in the cocoa powder until uniform, then whisk in the flour, oats, baking soda, and salt all at once until there are no undissolved bits of flour in the still-grainy batter. Using an offset spatula, spread the batter evenly into the prepared pan.

4. Bake until firm and set, and until a toothpick or cake tester inserted into the cake comes out clean, 22 to 24 minutes. Cool in the pan on a wire rack until room temperature, about 1½ hours.

For the buttercream

16 tablespoons (2 sticks) unsalted butter, melted
    and cooled to room temperature
1 cup unsweetened shredded coconut
⅔ cup unsweetened cocoa powder
⅔ cup whole or 2% milk
1 teaspoon vanilla extract
3 to 4 cups confectioners' sugar

1. Whisk the melted butter and coconut in a clean, dry, large bowl; then whisk in the cocoa powder until uniform.

2. Whisk in the milk and vanilla until smooth, then add 3 cups of the confectioners' sugar. Whisk until incorporated, adding more confectioners' sugar in 2-tablespoon increments until the frosting is thick and spreadable. Using an offset spatula, spread and smooth the frosting over the cooled cake.

TESTER NOTES
Use only powdery unsweetened shredded coconut for the right consistency in the frosting. If you have unsweetened coconut flakes, process about 1½ cups in the food processor until they're the consistency of powdered laundry detergent.

CHOCOLATE CHIP CAKE WITH PECAN-CARAMEL FROSTING

This one's actually a white cake with chocolate chips, fairly straightforward all 'round, with a little brown sugar and buttermilk to give it an unexpected depth of flavor. The frosting is superthick and sweet. Follow the instructions carefully. It's sort of like a layer of candy on top of the cake, a coconut-free riff on the stuff used between the layers of a traditional German chocolate cake.

For the cake

16 tablespoons (2 sticks) cool unsalted butter, cut into small chunks, plus additional for the sheet pan

3½ cups all-purpose flour, plus additional for the sheet pan

1 teaspoon baking powder

1 teaspoon baking soda

1 teaspoon salt

18 ounces semisweet or bittersweet chocolate chips

1 cup packed dark brown sugar

1 cup granulated white sugar

2 large eggs plus 2 large egg yolks

1 tablespoon vanilla extract

2 cups regular cultured buttermilk

1. Position the rack in the center of the oven. Heat the oven to 350°F. Generously butter and lightly flour the inside of a 13 x 18-inch lipped sheet pan.

2. Whisk 3 cups of the flour, the baking powder, baking soda, and salt in a medium bowl until uniform. Toss the remaining ½ cup flour with the chocolate chips in a small bowl.

3. Using a handheld electric mixer or a stand mixer with the paddle attachment, beat the butter and both sugars in a large bowl at medium speed until creamy, light, and fluffy, about 5 minutes. Beat in the eggs one at a time, then beat in the egg yolks one at a time, followed by the vanilla.

4. Turn off the mixer and pour the flour mixture evenly on top of the batter. Beat at low speed while slowly pouring in the buttermilk; continue beating until there are no bits of dry flour in the batter.

5. Scrape down and remove the beaters or paddle. Using a silicone spatula, fold in the coated chocolate chips and any residual flour in the bowl until well distributed. Using an offset spatula, scrape and spread the batter evenly into the prepared pan.

6. Bake until firm and set, and until a toothpick or cake tester inserted into the center of the cake comes out clean, 28 to 30 minutes. Cool in the pan on a wire rack until room temperature, about 2 hours.

For the frosting

2¼ cups granulated white sugar

20 tablespoons (2½ sticks) unsalted butter, cut into small chunks

1¼ cups evaporated whole milk (a little less than a 12-ounce can)

9 large egg yolks, at room temperature

2 tablespoons vanilla extract

¼ teaspoon salt

1¾ pounds pecan pieces (about 6 cups)

1. Whisk the sugar, butter, evaporated milk, egg yolks, vanilla, and salt in a medium saucepan set over medium heat until the butter melts. Continue cooking, whisking frequently, until bubbling. Then continue cooking, whisking nonstop, until thick and lightly caramel colored, about 10 minutes.

2. Stir in the pecan pieces and set aside for 2 minutes, stirring occasionally, until somewhat cool but still spreadable. Mound the mixture down the center of the cooled cake, then use an offset spatula to spread it into an even layer.

TESTER NOTES
Cool the frosting just until it won't singe the cake. But take care: if it gets too cool, you won't be able to spread it.

BROWNIE CAKE WITH DARK CHOCOLATE GLAZE

This sheet cake's got more butter and chocolate than we've ever used in a single recipe. (After developing over ten thousand recipes, that's saying something!) The whole thing's an absurd extravagance, designed almost to collapse under its own weight. The results are like a giant, dense, chewy brownie with a rich chocolate glaze. We felt a traditional frosting just went too far (although you may disagree and can search among other frostings in this book for one that suits your taste). We added pecans as a topping, if only to cut the richness.

For the cake
44 tablespoons (5½ sticks) unsalted butter, cut into small chunks, plus additional for the sheet pan

1¼ pounds chopped semisweet chocolate or semisweet chocolate chips

7 ounces unsweetened chocolate, chopped

1½ cups all-purpose flour, plus additional for the sheet pan

2 teaspoons baking powder

1 teaspoon salt

7 large eggs plus 1 large egg white, at room temperature

2 tablespoons vanilla extract

1¾ cups plus 1 tablespoon granulated white sugar

¾ cup plus 2 tablespoons packed dark brown sugar

1. Put the butter and both kinds of chocolate in a large saucepan set over very low heat. Stir until about three-quarters melted, then turn the heat off and continue stirring until smooth.

Set the pan off the element or burner and cool to room temperature, about 30 minutes.

2. Position the rack in the center of the oven. Heat the oven to 350°F. Generously butter and lightly flour the inside of a 13 x 18-inch lipped sheet pan.

3. Whisk the flour, baking powder, and salt in a medium bowl until uniform.

4. Scrape the cooled chocolate mixture into a large bowl. Using a handheld electric mixer or a stand mixer with the whisk attachment, beat in the eggs at medium speed one at a time.

5. Beat in the egg white and vanilla until smooth. Then beat in both sugars until very luxurious and uniform, about 3 minutes.

6. Stop the mixer, scrape down the inside of the bowl, and add the flour mixture. Beat at very low speed just until there's no dry flour in the bowl, particularly at the bottom. Using an offset spatula, spread the thick batter evenly into the prepared pan.

7. Bake until set to the touch and slightly puffed, and until a toothpick or cake tester inserted into the center of the cake comes out with a few moist crumbs attached, 25 to 28 minutes. Cool in the pan on a wire rack to room temperature, about 2 hours.

For the glaze

9 tablespoons water
3 tablespoons dark corn syrup
4 ounces unsweetened chocolate, chopped
1 teaspoon vanilla extract
3½ to 4 cups confectioners' sugar
3 cups (about 13 ounces) chopped pecans,
    for topping

1. Bring the water and corn syrup to a boil in a small saucepan set over medium heat, stirring several times at the beginning. Boil for 1 minute undisturbed. Remove from the heat.

2. Put the chocolate in a large heat-safe bowl; pour the hot sugar syrup on top. Stir until the chocolate has melted and the mixture is smooth. Stir in the vanilla.

3. Stir in 3 cups of the confectioners' sugar until dissolved, then stir in another ¼ cup. Keep stirring in more confectioners' sugar in 2-tablespoon increments until you have a thick, dark, spreadable glaze, not a frosting. Cool for 5 minutes, then use an offset spatula to spread and smooth this glaze over the cooled cake. Sprinkle the top with chopped pecans before serving.

TESTER NOTES

For more flavor, toast the pecan pieces or halves on a large sheet pan in a 300°F oven for about 8 minutes, stirring often, until lightly browned and aromatic. Cool to room temperature before chopping and using.

BOSTON CREAM CAKE

Like a Boston cream pie, here's a vanilla cake underneath, a creamy vanilla pudding over that, and a chocolate glaze, all recombined as a sheet cake with three distinct layers. The only trick is getting the temperature of the upper parts right. The pudding must be cold and set before it's spread into place; the chocolate glaze, truly at room temperature so as not to melt the pudding.

3 cups whole milk
2 tablespoons vanilla extract
2½ cups plus 2 tablespoons granulated white
    sugar
5 large eggs plus 6 large egg yolks, at room
    temperature
½ cup cornstarch
½ teaspoon salt
20 tablespoons (2½ sticks) cool unsalted butter,
    cut into small chunks, plus additional for the
    sheet pan
2½ cups all-purpose flour
2 teaspoons baking powder
1¾ cup plus ⅓ cup heavy cream
2 tablespoons light corn syrup
12 ounces chopped bittersweet chocolate or
    bittersweet chocolate chips

1. Heat the milk and 1 tablespoon of the vanilla in a medium saucepan set over medium-low heat until small bubbles fizz around the inside perimeter of the pan.

2. Using a handheld electric mixer or a whisk, beat ¾ cup of the sugar and the 6 egg yolks in a large bowl at medium speed until you can make wide ribbons, about 5 minutes. (It'll take up to 10 minutes with a whisk.)

3. Beat or whisk in the cornstarch and ¼ teaspoon of the salt until smooth. Beating at medium speed or whisking steadily, add about two-thirds of the hot milk mixture in a slow, steady stream. Then beat or whisk this combined mixture back into the remaining milk mixture in the saucepan until smooth.

4. Set the pan over medium-low heat and cook, whisking constantly, just until bubbling and thickened, about 2 minutes.

5. Pour the pudding into a large bowl, cover with plastic wrap by pressing the wrap right against the hot pudding, and refrigerate for at least 6 hours or overnight.

6. Position the rack in the center of the oven. Heat the oven to 350°F. Generously butter the inside of a 13 x 18-inch lipped sheet pan.

7. Whisk the flour, baking powder, and remaining ¼ teaspoon salt in a medium bowl until uniform.

8. Using a handheld electric mixer with clean, dry beaters or a stand mixer with the paddle attachment, beat the butter and the remaining 1¾ cups plus 2 tablespoons sugar in a large bowl at medium speed until creamy, light, and fluffy, about 5 minutes.

9. Beat in the whole eggs one at a time, then scrape down the inside of the bowl and beat in ¾ cup of the cream and the remaining 1 tablespoon vanilla.

10. Turn off the mixer, add the flour mixture, and beat at low speed to form a very thick batter with no dry specks remaining, particularly at the bottom of the bowl. Using an offset spatula, spread the thick batter evenly into the prepared pan.

11. Bake until lightly browned and set, and until a toothpick or cake tester inserted into the center of the cake comes out clean, 18 to 20 minutes. Cool in the pan on a wire rack to room temperature, about 1½ hours.

12. Heat the remaining 1⅓ cups cream and the corn syrup in a small saucepan set over medium-low heat, stirring constantly for about a minute and then undisturbed thereafter, until small bubbles fizz around the inside perimeter of the pan.

13. Put the chocolate in a heat-safe medium bowl. Pour the hot cream mixture over the chocolate, then whisk until smooth. Set aside to cool to room temperature, whisking occasionally, just until thick enough to pour but not run everywhere, 10 to 15 minutes.

14. Using an offset spatula, spread and smooth the pudding layer over the cooled cake. Pour the cooled chocolate glaze over the pudding, spreading it gently and evenly with that same offset spatula. Refrigerate for at least 1 hour or up to 1 day before serving.

CHOCOLATE SPONGE CAKE WITH MARSHMALLOW FROSTING

This slightly chewy dessert is really a classic sponge cake revamped to be a crowd-pleasing sheet cake. It's fairly straightforward, so it needs a thick, decadent frosting to give it some oomph. This marshmallow concoction has all the texture of soft candy without any of the fuss of candy making, thanks to that childhood standard, marshmallow creme.

For the cake
¾ cup canola or vegetable oil, plus additional for the sheet pan
1 cup whole milk
¾ cup unsweetened cocoa powder
1¾ cups cake flour
1½ cups granulated white sugar
2 teaspoons baking powder
½ teaspoon salt
6 large eggs, separated, plus 2 large whites, at room temperature
½ teaspoon cream of tartar
1 tablespoon vanilla extract

1. Position the rack in the center of the oven. Heat the oven to 350°F. Generously oil the inside of a 13 x 18-inch lipped sheet pan.

2. Heat the milk in a small saucepan set over medium heat until small bubbles fizz around the inside perimeter of the pan. Remove from the heat, whisk in the cocoa powder until smooth, pour into a medium bowl, and cool for 30 minutes.

3. Meanwhile, whisk the flour, sugar, baking powder, and salt in a large bowl until uniform. Set aside.

4. Using a handheld electric mixer or a stand mixer with the whisk attachment, beat the 8 egg whites in a second large bowl at medium speed until foamy. Add the cream of tartar, increase the speed to high, and continue beating until you can make soft peaks. Set aside.

5. Whisk the oil, 6 egg yolks, and vanilla into the cooled milk mixture until smooth, almost creamy, about 2 minutes.

6. Make a well in the center of the flour mixture. Pour the milk mixture into it and whisk until smooth and thick. Use a silicone spatula to fold the egg white mixture into the batter, using slow, steady, and gentle arcs to get it incorporated without losing the whites' loft. There may be white streaks remaining. Pour the fairly wet batter evenly into the prepared pan and smooth it out evenly with an offset spatula.

7. Bake until puffed and set, about 25 minutes. Cool in the pan on a wire rack to room temperature, about 2 hours. The cake will deflate and pull away from the pan's sides as it cools.

For the frosting

¾ cup solid vegetable shortening
9 tablespoons (1 stick plus 1 tablespoon) unsalted butter, softened to room temperature
2½ to 3½ cups confectioners' sugar
2 tablespoons vanilla extract
½ teaspoon salt
1 cup marshmallow creme, such as Marshmallow Fluff

1. Using a handheld electric mixer or a stand mixer with the paddle attachment, beat the shortening and butter at medium speed in a large bowl until creamy, about 2 minutes.

2. Turn off the mixer and add 2 cups of the confectioners' sugar. Beat at low speed until thick and smooth. Increase the speed to medium, adding more confectioners' sugar as necessary in 2-tablespoon increments, until the frosting is spreadable and can hold its shape on the side of a spatula.

3. Beat in the vanilla and salt until smooth, then beat in the marshmallow creme until uniform. Using an offset spatula, spread and smooth the frosting over the cooled cake.

TESTER NOTES

The cake is a classic sponge: springy, not very high in the pan. Don't be tempted to add more leavening. This one's ultimately more frosting than cake!

CO'-COLA CAKE WITH MARASCHINO CHERRY FROSTING

If you're from the South, you'll know what we're talking about: a light, airy, almost springy chocolate cake made with cola (or co'-cola in the local parlance). Our version is topped with a frosting made from the liquid in a jar of maraschino cherries. You might call it a cherry Coke sheet cake.

For the cake

10 tablespoons (1 stick plus 2 tablespoons) unsalted butter, plus additional for the sheet pan

3⅓ cups all-purpose flour, plus additional for the sheet pan

9 ounces chopped semisweet chocolate or semisweet chocolate chips

1½ teaspoons baking powder

½ teaspoon salt

¾ cup granulated white sugar

⅔ cup whole or 2% milk

2 large eggs, at room temperature

1 tablespoon vanilla extract

One 12-ounce bottle room-temperature, regular Coca-Cola or cola-flavored soda (do not use diet soda)

1. Position the rack in the center of the oven. Heat the oven to 350°F. Generously butter and lightly flour the inside of a 13 x 18-inch lipped sheet pan.

2. Put the chocolate and butter in a medium saucepan; stir over very low heat until about two-thirds of the chocolate has melted. Remove the pan from the heat and continue stirring until smooth. Scrape the mixture into a large bowl and cool to room temperature, about 20 minutes.

3. Whisk the flour, baking powder, and salt in a medium bowl until uniform.

4. Whisk the sugar, milk, eggs, and vanilla into the melted chocolate mixture until smooth. Add half the flour mixture and whisk until dissolved. Pour in the cola, whisk well, and then add the remaining flour mixture. Whisk just until there are no bits of dry flour in the batter. Using an offset spatula, spread the batter evenly into the prepared pan.

5. Bake until set to the touch and somewhat puffed, and until a toothpick or cake tester inserted into the center of the cake comes out clean, about 17 minutes. Cool in the pan on a wire rack to room temperature, about 1½ hours.

For the frosting

8 tablespoons (1 stick) unsalted butter, softened to room temperature

3 to 4 cups confectioners' sugar

½ cup heavy cream

⅓ cup syrup from a large jar of maraschino cherries, plus the drained maraschino cherries for topping

1 teaspoon vanilla extract

1. Using a handheld electric mixer or a stand mixer with the whisk attachment, beat the butter and 2 cups of the confectioners' sugar in a large bowl at low speed for 1 minute. Increase the speed to medium and beat until smooth, about 1 more minute.

2. Add the cream, maraschino syrup, and vanilla; beat at medium speed until smooth. Turn off the mixer, add 1 cup confectioners' sugar, and beat at low speed until combined.

3. Increase the speed to medium and beat, adding confectioners' sugar in ¼-cup increments, until the frosting is spreadable and can hold its shape on the side of a spatula. Spread and smooth the frosting over the top of the cake. Just before serving, top the cake with drained maraschino cherries.

TESTER NOTES
This is a great cake to cut into circles and frost like little individual layer cakes. Use a 3- or 4-inch round cookie cutter.

CHOCOLATE DOUBLE-MALTED CAKE

You know the bad thing about chocolate? When it's sweetened too much, it loses its subtle, bitter notes, those reminiscent of dark coffee, toffee, or toasted nuts. To remedy that problem, we used only unsweetened chocolate in the batter for this sheet cake. Then we added milk chocolate chips for a sweet finish. Oh, and we added lots of malt, too, even in the frosting. We wanted its nutty, wheaty sweetness to go head-to-head with all that chocolate.

For the cake
10 tablespoons (1¼ sticks) unsalted butter, cut into small chunks, plus additional for the sheet pan
5 ounces unsweetened chocolate, chopped
3 cups all-purpose flour
2 teaspoons baking powder
½ teaspoon salt
1½ cups whole or 2% milk
1 cup plus 2 tablespoons malted milk powder
3 large eggs, at room temperature
1½ cups granulated white sugar
2 teaspoons vanilla extract
12 ounces milk chocolate chips

1. Position the rack in the center of the oven. Heat the oven to 350°F. Generously butter the inside of a 13 x 18-inch lipped sheet pan.

2. Place the butter and chocolate in a medium saucepan set over low heat. Stir until about three-quarters of the chocolate has melted. Remove the pan from the heat and continue stirring until smooth. Cool for 20 minutes.

3. Whisk the flour, baking powder, and salt in a medium bowl until uniform. Whisk the milk and malted milk powder in a second medium bowl until the powder dissolves.

4. Using a handheld electric mixer or a stand mixer with the whisk attachment, beat the eggs and sugar in a large bowl at medium speed until you can make wide ribbons. (The mixture will almost double in volume.) Beat in the cooled butter mixture and the vanilla until smooth.

5. Turn off the mixer and pour the flour mixture evenly over the batter. Beating at low speed, slowly pour in the milk mixture; continue beating until there are no bits of dry flour in the batter. Add the chocolate chips and beat just until evenly distributed. Using an offset spatula, spread the thick batter evenly into the prepared pan.

6. Bake until firm to the touch, and until a toothpick or cake tester inserted into the center of the cake comes out clean, 20 to 24 minutes. Cool in the pan on a wire rack to room temperature, about 1½ hours.

For the buttercream

24 tablespoons (3 sticks) unsalted butter, softened to room temperature
¾ cup malted milk powder
2 tablespoons heavy cream
2 teaspoons vanilla extract
2 to 3 cups confectioners' sugar
2 cups malted milk balls, crushed, for topping

1. Using a handheld electric mixer or a stand mixer with the whisk attachment, beat the butter and malted milk powder in a large bowl at medium speed until creamy and light, about 2 minutes. Beat in the cream and vanilla until smooth.

2. Turn off the mixer and add 2 cups of the confectioners' sugar. Beat at low speed until smooth; then beat at medium speed, adding more confectioners' sugar in ¼-cup increments, until the frosting is spreadable and can hold its shape on the side of a spatula. Using an offset spatula, spread and smooth the frosting evenly over the cooled cake. Sprinkle the crushed malted milk balls on top before serving.

TESTER NOTES
Use malted milk powder, not diastatic malt powder.

GLUTEN-FREE FUDGY CAKE WITH VEGAN CHOCOLATE FROSTING

Avocados in a frosting? Stick with us. They give it a rich depth of flavor, especially when paired with chocolate. We matched this unusual frosting to this cake because we loved the rich flavor and supercreamy texture that frosting brought to the dense cake, similar to the flourless chocolate cakes popular in so many restaurants. Unfortunately, the frosting won't keep long on the cake, so plan on serving this one the day you make it. Feel free, of course, to mix and match the cake to any frosting in the book that suits your taste. Or use this vegan frosting on any egg-free, dairy-free cake in the book for a vegan dessert.

For the cake

10 tablespoons (1¼ sticks) unsalted butter, cut into small chunks, plus additional for the sheet pan
12 ounces chopped bittersweet chocolate or bittersweet chocolate chips
8 large eggs, separated, at room temperature
1 cup granulated white sugar
1 cup heavy cream
½ cup unsweetened cocoa powder
¼ cup cornstarch

1. Position the rack in the center of the oven. Heat the oven to 350°F. Generously butter the inside of a 13 x 18-inch lipped sheet pan.

2. Set the chocolate and butter in a medium saucepan over low heat and melt, stirring quite often, until smooth. Do not let the mixture bubble. Set aside off the heat and cool to room temperature, about 30 minutes, stirring once in a while.

3. Put the egg whites in a dry large bowl. Using a handheld electric mixer or a stand mixer with the whisk attachment, beat at low speed until foamy, then at high speed until you can make droopy peaks. Beat in the sugar at high speed 1 tablespoon at a time. Continue beating until you can make glossy, firm peaks.

4. Whisk the egg yolks and cream in a second large bowl until smooth and even a little light, about 3 minutes. Whisk in the cocoa powder and cornstarch until dissolved, about 1 minute.

5. Using a silicone spatula, fold in the melted chocolate mixture until uniform. Then fold in half the beaten egg white mixture until smooth. Add the remaining egg white mixture and fold in wide, gentle arcs, just until incorporated (although there may be white streaks in the batter). Using an offset spatula, spread the batter evenly into the prepared pan.

6. Bake until puffed and set, and until a toothpick or cake tester inserted into the center of the cake comes out clean, about 20 minutes. Cool in the pan on a wire rack to room temperature, about 1½ hours.

For the frosting

4 very ripe, soft avocados, peeled and pitted
⅔ cup unsweetened cocoa powder
½ teaspoon vanilla extract
½ teaspoon salt
3 to 4 cups confectioners' sugar

1. Using a flatware fork or a potato masher, mash the avocados in a large bowl until smooth (no lumps at all, about like baby food). Stir in the cocoa powder, vanilla, and salt. Scrape down and remove the utensil.

2. Add 3 cups of the confectioners' sugar. Whisk until thick and smooth, adding more confectioners' sugar in 2-tablespoon increments until the mixture is spreadable and can hold its shape on the whisk. Using an offset spatula, spread and smooth the frosting over the cooled cake.

TESTER NOTES

Since the cake is gluten-free, its structure will be created almost entirely by air—that is, both by whisking the egg yolks with the cream and by beating the egg whites with the sugar. The more air you can get into these mixtures, the more tender the final crumb of the cake.

CHOCOLATE–PEANUT BUTTER CAKE WITH CHOCOLATE WHIPPED CREAM

Here, we get a dense, firm texture by adding melted butter to the batter, rather than creaming cold butter with the sugar at the start. We beat less air into the batter and end up with a cake that can stand up to this chocolate whipped cream, actually a cooked confection, sort of like a fluffy, marshmallowy meringue.

For the cake

12 tablespoons (1½ sticks) unsalted butter, melted and cooled, plus additional for the sheet pan
1½ cups all-purpose flour, plus additional for the sheet pan
⅓ cup unsweetened cocoa powder
1 teaspoon ground cinnamon
1 teaspoon baking soda
½ teaspoon salt
2 cups granulated white sugar
¾ cup natural-style creamy peanut butter
2 large eggs, at room temperature
2 teaspoons vanilla extract
1½ cups regular cultured buttermilk

1. Position the rack in the center of the oven. Heat the oven to 350°F. Generously butter and lightly flour a 13 x 18-inch lipped sheet pan.

2. Whisk the flour, cocoa powder, cinnamon, baking soda, and salt in a medium bowl until uniform.

3. Using a handheld electric mixer or a stand mixer with the paddle attachment, beat the sugar and peanut butter in a large bowl at medium speed until velvety, about 3 minutes. Beat in the eggs one at a time. Pour in the melted butter and vanilla; beat until smooth.

4. Turn off the mixer; add a third of the flour mixture. Beat at low speed just until combined. Beat in half the buttermilk, then half of the remaining flour mixture until evenly distributed. Beat in the remaining buttermilk. Scrape down and remove the beaters or paddle. Using a silicone spatula, fold in the remaining flour just until there are no dry pockets of flour in the slightly grainy batter. Pour and spread this mixture into the prepared pan.

5. Bake until set to the touch, and until a toothpick or cake tester inserted into the center of the cake comes out clean, about 20 minutes. Cool in the pan on a wire rack to room temperature, about 2 hours.

For the chocolate whipped cream
3½ cups heavy cream
½ cup confectioners' sugar
1 tablespoon cornstarch
7 tablespoons *sifted* unsweetened cocoa powder
Chocolate sprinkles or jimmies, for topping

1. Whisking all the while, heat 1 cup of the heavy cream, the confectioners' sugar, and cornstarch in a small saucepan set over medium heat until bubbling and thickened. Remove the pan from the heat and cool to room temperature, about 1 hour.

2. Using a handheld electric mixer or a stand mixer with the whisk attachment, beat the remaining 2½ cups cream and the sifted cocoa powder in a large bowl at high speed until the mixture thickens enough that the turned-off beaters can leave tracks in it.

3. Beating all the while at medium speed, drizzle in the cooled cornstarch mixture, then continue beating until the mixture can form stiff peaks on the side of a silicone spatula. Using that spatula, spread the chocolate whipped cream over the cooled cake. Scatter chocolate sprinkles across the top before serving.

TESTER NOTES
You must sift the cocoa powder for the whipped cream. Measure it *after* sifting. Little clumps won't dissolve in the mix and can end up scattered throughout the frosting.

VANILLA CAKE WITH CONFETTI FROSTING

Since we've covered chocolate cakes pretty well, let's turn to a real classic: a slab of buttery vanilla bliss. You can make this cake incredibly light, almost airy, if you beat that butter and sugar until they're thick and fluffy. (You think you're done? You're not.) If you put enough air into them before you add the flour, the cake's going to rise up high in the sheet pan. Make sure yours has 1-inch edges all around.

For the vanilla cake

32 tablespoons (4 sticks) cool unsalted butter, cut into small chunks, plus additional for the sheet pan
3½ cups cake flour, plus additional for the pan
1 teaspoon baking powder
½ teaspoon salt
2 cups granulated white sugar
10 large eggs, at room temperature
1 tablespoon vanilla extract

1. Position the rack in the center of the oven. Heat the oven to 350°F. Generously butter and lightly flour the inside of a 13 x 18-inch lipped sheet pan.

2. Whisk the flour, baking powder, and salt in a medium bowl until uniform.

3. Using a handheld electric mixer or a stand mixer with the paddle attachment, beat the butter and sugar in a large bowl at medium speed until light and fluffy, about 6 minutes.

4. Scrape down the inside of the bowl, then beat in the eggs one at a time. Beat in the vanilla until smooth.

5. Scrape down and remove the beaters or paddle. Using a silicone spatula, fold in the flour mixture just until there are no dry bits of flour in the batter. Use an offset spatula to spread the thick batter evenly into the prepared pan.

6. Bake until lightly browned and set, and until a toothpick or cake tester inserted into the center of the cake comes out clean, 24 to 26 minutes. Cool in the pan on a wire rack to room temperature, about 2 hours.

For the frosting

12 tablespoons (1½ sticks) unsalted butter, softened to room temperature
4 to 5 cups confectioners' sugar
¾ cup heavy cream
6 tablespoons light corn syrup
1 tablespoon vanilla extract
½ teaspoon salt
Rainbow cake sprinkles or jimmies, for topping

1. Using a handheld electric mixer or a stand mixer with the whisk attachment, beat the butter and 3 cups of the confectioners' sugar in a large bowl at low speed until well blended and smooth.

2. Add ½ cup confectioners' sugar as well as the cream, corn syrup, vanilla, and salt. Beat at medium speed until thick and spreadable, adding more confectioners' sugar in ¼ -cup increments until the frosting is thick enough to hold its shape on the side of a spatula. Using an offset spatula, spread and smooth the frosting over the cooled cake. Scatter the rainbow sprinkles across the top before serving.

TESTER NOTES
Add sprinkles or jimmies just before serving.

VANILLA SPONGE CAKE WITH
BLACKBERRY–SOUR CREAM FROSTING

A sponge cake is all about texture: slightly chewy, even a little springy. It's missing the standard, grainy crumb of a sheet cake. It's like a denser version of angel food cake. (There are all those egg yolks, after all, to make it cakier.) This one will puff up a bit, then fall back, flatten out, and pull away from the pan's sides as it cools.

For the cake

½ cup canola or vegetable oil, plus additonal for
  the sheet pan
2 cups cake flour
1½ cups granulated white sugar
1 tablespoon baking powder
1 teaspoon salt
9 large eggs, separated, at room temperature
½ teaspoon cream of tartar
1 cup whole milk
2 teaspoons vanilla extract

1. Position the rack in the center of the oven. Heat the oven to 375°F. Generously oil the inside of a 13 x 18-inch lipped sheet pan.

2. Whisk the flour, sugar, baking powder, and salt in a large bowl until uniform.

3. Using a handheld electric mixer or a stand mixer with the whisk attachment, beat the egg whites in a second large bowl at low speed until foamy. Add the cream of tartar, increase the speed to high, and beat until you can make soft droopy peaks on the side of a silicone spatula.

4. Whisk the milk, oil, egg yolks, and vanilla in a medium bowl until smooth and even a bit creamy, about 2 minutes.

5. Make a well in the center of the prepared flour mixture, pour in the milk mixture, and whisk until smooth. Use a silicone spatula to fold in the egg white mixture in steady, even arcs, just until combined, even if there are still white streaks. Using an offset spatula, spread the batter evenly into the prepared pan.

6. Bake until puffed, set, and lightly browned, 15 to 18 minutes. Cool in the pan to room temperature, about 1½ hours.

For the frosting

4½ to 6 cups confectioners' sugar
16 tablespoons (2 sticks) unsalted butter,
  softened to room temperature
8 ounces full-fat sour cream
¾ cup seedless blackberry jam
2 teaspoons vanilla extract
Fresh blackberries, for topping

1. Using a handheld electric mixer or a stand mixer with the whisk attachment, beat 3½ cups of the confections' sugar and the butter in a large bowl at low speed for about 1 minute, then increase the speed to medium and continue beating until smooth and uniform.

2. Add the sour cream, jam, and vanilla; beat at medium speed until well blended. Continue beating, adding more confectioners' sugar in ¼-cup increments until the frosting is spreadable but thick enough to hold its shape on the side of a spatula.

3. Using an offset spatula, spread and smooth the frosting evenly over the cooled cake. Cut into servings and top each with fresh blackberries.

BUTTERMILK CAKE WITH PEANUT BUTTER FROSTING

You've got to tame the rich, salty flavor of this peanut butter frosting somehow! The sour buttermilk gives this cake not only a brighter flavor but also a bit of lofty lightness, particularly when used with cake flour. But it's not too light. This dessert's still all about the smooth, rich frosting on top. If you want, top it all with chopped salted peanuts.

For the cake

16 tablespoons (2 sticks) cool unsalted butter, cut into small chunks, plus additional for the sheet pan
3 cups cake flour, plus additional for the sheet pan
1 tablespoon baking soda
¾ teaspoon baking powder
¾ teaspoon salt
1 cup granulated white sugar
3 large eggs, at room temperature
1½ teaspoons vanilla extract
1½ cups regular cultured buttermilk

1. Position the rack in the center of the oven. Heat the oven to 350°F. Generously butter and lightly flour a 13 x 18-inch lipped sheet pan.

2. Whisk the flour, baking soda, baking powder, and salt in a medium bowl until uniform.

3. Using a handheld electric mixer or a stand mixer with the paddle attachment, beat the butter and sugar in a large bowl at medium speed until light and fluffy, about 5 minutes. Beat in the eggs one at a time, followed by the vanilla.

4. Turn off the mixer and pour the flour mixture evenly on top of the batter. Beat at low speed while slowly pouring in the buttermilk; continue beating until there are no bits of dry flour in the batter. Using an offset spatula, spread the batter evenly into the prepared pan.

5. Bake until golden and set to the touch, and until a toothpick or cake tester inserted into the center of the cake comes out clean, 15 to 17 minutes. Cool in the pan on a wire rack to room temperature, about 2 hours.

For the frosting

1½ cups standard-style smooth peanut butter
5 tablespoons unsalted butter, softened to room temperature
½ cup light cream
1 tablespoon vanilla extract
4 to 5 cups confectioners' sugar

1. Using a handheld electric mixer or a stand mixer with the whisk attachment, beat the peanut butter and butter in a large bowl at medium speed until smooth and creamy. Add the cream and vanilla; continue beating at medium speed until smooth.

2. Turn off the mixer and add 3½ cups of the confectioners' sugar. Beat at low speed until combined; then beat at medium speed, adding more confectioners' sugar in ¼-cup increments until the frosting is spreadable and will hold its shape on the side of a spatula. Using an offset spatula, spread and smooth the frosting evenly over the cooled cake.

M&M WHITE CAKE WITH CREAM CHEESE FROSTING AND GORP

Seriously, does anyone eat "good old raisins and peanuts" without M&Ms anymore? So here's a sheet cake to represent: a buttery white cake with lots of M&Ms.

For the cake

23 tablespoons (2 sticks plus 7 tablespoons) unsalted butter, cut into small chunks, plus additional for the sheet pan
2¾ cups all-purpose flour, plus additional for the sheet pan
2 teaspoons baking powder
½ teaspoon salt
2⅔ cups granulated white sugar
4 large eggs plus 1 large egg white
1 cup plus 2 tablespoons whole or 2% milk
One 11.4-ounce bag plain milk chocolate M&M candies (about 2 cups)

1. Position the rack in the center of the oven. Heat the oven to 350°F. Generously butter and lightly flour a 13 x 18-inch lipped sheet pan.

2. Whisk the flour, baking powder, and salt in a medium bowl until uniform.

3. Using a handheld electric mixer or a stand mixer with the paddle attachment, beat the butter and sugar in a large bowl at medium speed until fluffy, about 5 minutes. Beat in the eggs one a time, then the egg white.

4. Turn off the mixer and pour the flour mixture evenly on top of the batter. Beat at low speed while slowly pouring in the milk, until all the flour is moistened, even if the batter is still

grainy. Use an offset spatula to spread the batter evenly into the prepared pan. Sprinkle the M&Ms on top.

5. Bake until lightly browned and set and a toothpick or cake tester inserted into the center of the cake comes out clean, 30 to 35 minutes. Cool in the pan on a wire rack to room temperature, about 2 hours.

For the frosting and GORP

12 ounces full-fat cream cheese, at room temperature
8 tablespoons (1 stick) unsalted butter, at room temperature
½ cup light corn syrup
2 teaspoons vanilla extract
2½ to 4 cups confectioners' sugar
1¼ cups salted roasted peanuts, for topping
1¼ cups raisins, for topping

1. Using a handheld electric mixer or a stand mixer with the whisk attachment, beat the cream cheese, butter, corn syrup, and vanilla in a large bowl at medium-high speed until smooth and creamy, about 3 minutes.

2. Beat in 2 cups of the confectioners' sugar at low speed until smooth, then keep beating in more confectioners' sugar, starting with ½ cup and adding less and less each time, until the frosting is thick and can hold its shape on the side of a spatula.

3. Using an offset spatula, spread and smooth the frosting over the cooled cake. Sprinkle the peanuts and raisins on top just before serving.

BACON–PEANUT BUTTER CAKE
WITH MAPLE BUTTERCREAM

We've used more than a pound of bacon (!) to create one of the most intense desserts in this book: the cooked bacon bits get folded into the batter, which is also made with the rendered fat. It all comes together as a dense and substantial cake, the right base for this rich buttercream. Don't even think about using pancake syrup instead of real maple syrup for this non-traditional buttercream with cream cheese in the mix. It's exceptionally rich. If we're using so much bacon, why not?

For the cake

At least 4 tablespoons (½ stick) unsalted butter, cut into small chunks, plus additional for the sheet pan

3¼ cups all-purpose flour, plus additional for the sheet pan

1¼ pounds thin-cut bacon, roughly chopped

1 tablespoon baking powder

1½ teaspoons baking soda

½ teaspoon salt

1 cup packed dark brown sugar

⅔ cup natural-style creamy peanut butter

½ cup honey

4 large eggs, at room temperature

1 tablespoon vanilla extract

1½ cups regular cultured buttermilk

1. Position the rack in the center of the oven. Heat the oven to 350°F. Generously butter and lightly flour the inside of a 13 x 18-inch lipped sheet pan.

2. Fry the bacon in a large skillet set over medium heat until crisp, almost like bacon bits. Remove the skillet from the heat; use a slotted spoon to transfer the bacon bits to a plate. Do not discard the rendered fat. Cool for 5 minutes.

3. Meanwhile, pour the rendered bacon fat into a heat-safe (Pyrex) measuring cup. Add ¼ cup butter (½ stick) and let it melt. Add more butter if necessary until you have 1 cup total melted fat. Cool for 5 more minutes.

4. Whisk the flour, baking powder, baking soda, and salt in a medium bowl until uniform. Set ⅓ cup bacon bits aside for a topping.

5. Using a handheld electric mixer or a stand mixer with the paddle attachment, beat the bacon fat–butter mixture, brown sugar, peanut butter, and honey in a large bowl at medium speed until light and smooth, about 5 minutes. Scrape down the inside of the bowl, then beat in the eggs one at a time. Beat in the vanilla until smooth and uniform.

6. Stop the mixer and scrape down the bowl again. Pour the flour mixture evenly over the egg mixture. Beating at low speed, pour in the buttermilk in a slow, steady stream. Beat in the larger portion of the bacon bits, just until all the flour has been moistened. Using an offset spatula, spread the batter evenly into the prepared pan.

7. Bake until puffed and golden brown, and until a toothpick or cake tester inserted into the center of the cake comes out clean, about 25 minutes. Cool in the pan to room temperature, about 2 hours.

For the buttercream

16 tablespoons (2 sticks) unsalted butter, softened to room temperature
8 ounces full-fat cream cheese, softened to room temperature
1½ to 2 cups confectioners' sugar
1 cup maple syrup, preferably Grade A robust, Grade B, or Grade 2
½ teaspoon salt
2 large egg yolks, at room temperature

1. Using a handheld electric mixer or a stand mixer with the whisk attachment, beat the butter, cream cheese, and 1 cup of the confectioners' sugar in a large bowl at medium speed until creamy and light, about 2 minutes. Beat in the maple syrup and salt until smooth, then beat in the egg yolks until uniform.

2. Continue beating, adding more confectioners' sugar in 2-tablespoon increments, until the frosting is spreadable and can hold its shape on the side of a spatula.

3. Using an offset spatula, spread and smooth the frosting evenly over the cooled cake. Sprinkle the reserved ⅓ cup bacon bits on top.

TESTER NOTES

This buttercream uses raw egg yolks for richness. If this is a concern for health or safety reasons, simply omit them, although you may then need about ½ cup less confectioners' sugar than we recommend. Or search out farm-fresh eggs at an organic stand. Or use pasteurized in-the-shell eggs, available at many large supermarkets.

SCOTTISH OAT CAKE WITH SOUR CREAM FROSTING

What do a Scottish oat cake, a cream scone, and an American sheet cake have in common? This recipe! It's a hybrid among them. The resulting cake is dense, robust, and even a little chewy, thanks to the oats. It gets topped with a light frosting, a combination of whipped cream and sour cream.

For the cake

10½ tablespoons (1 stick plus 2½ tablespoons) cool unsalted butter, cut into small chunks, plus additional for the sheet pan
1 cup whole or 2% milk
1⅓ cups rolled oats
2 cups all-purpose flour
1½ teaspoons baking soda
½ teaspoon salt
1 cup granulated white sugar
1 cup packed light brown sugar
2 large eggs plus 1 large egg white, at room temperature
1 cup regular cultured buttermilk

1. Position the rack in the center of the oven. Heat the oven to 350°F. Generously butter the inside of a 13 x 18-inch lipped sheet pan.

2. Warm the milk in a medium saucepan set over medium heat until small bubbles fizz around the inside perimeter of the pan. Stir in the oats, cover, and set aside for 1 hour.

3. Whisk the flour, baking soda, and salt in a medium bowl until uniform.

4. Using a handheld electric mixer or a stand mixer with the paddle attachment, beat the butter and both sugars in a large bowl at medium speed until light, fluffy, and creamy, about 5 minutes. Scrape down the inside of the bowl and beat in the eggs one at a time.

5. Beat in the egg white until smooth and uniform. Add the oat mixture and beat at low speed until well combined. Scrape down and remove the beaters or paddle.

6. Using a silicone spatula, fold in a third of the flour mixture, then half the buttermilk until smooth. Fold in half the remaining flour mixture, then the remaining buttermilk, just until the flour has dissolved. Finally, fold in the remaining flour mixture just until there are no dry specks of flour in the batter. Using an offset spatula, spread the thick batter evenly into the prepared pan.

7. Bake until lightly browned and set, and until a toothpick or cake tester inserted into the center of the cake comes out clean, about 18 minutes. Cool in the pan on a wire rack to room temperature, about 1½ hours.

For the frosting

2 cups cold heavy cream
1 cup full-fat sour cream
2 teaspoons vanilla extract
2 cups confectioners' sugar

1. Pour the cream into a large bowl. Using a handheld electric mixer or a stand mixer with the whisk attachment, beat at high speed until you can form stiff peaks, about 2 minutes. Scrape down and remove the beaters or whisk.

2. Whisk the sour cream and vanilla in a second large bowl. Whisk in the confectioners' sugar until smooth.

3. Using a silicone spatula, fold in the beaten whipped cream without deflating it, until smooth and moundable. Using an offset spatula, spread the frosting over the cooled cake.

TESTER NOTES

Because of the oats, the cake won't keep well after the first day at room temperature. But it does freeze well *before* frosting. Once cooled, cut it into quarters or even smaller pieces, wrap them individually, and freeze for up to four months.

JAM THUMBPRINT CAKE

Some things are just waiting to be made. This one's our take on the old-school cookie. We can't sprinkle nuts across the cake (as we might for those cookies). The cake takes too long to bake; the nuts will singe and turn bitter. However, we can use coconut for a crunchy topping along with the jam.

32 tablespoons (4 sticks) cool unsalted butter, cut into small chunks, plus additional for the sheet pan
4⅔ cups all-purpose flour
1½ teaspoons baking powder
¼ teaspoon salt
1⅓ cups granulated white sugar
2 large eggs plus 1 large egg white, at room temperature
2½ cups sweetened shredded coconut
1½ cups jam, such as raspberry, blackberry, apricot, or strawberry

1. Position the rack in the center of the oven. Heat the oven to 350°F. Generously butter the inside of a 13 x 18-inch lipped sheet pan.

2. Whisk the flour, baking powder, and salt in a medium bowl until uniform.

3. Using a handheld electric mixer or a stand mixer with the paddle attachment, beat the butter and sugar in a large bowl at medium speed until creamy and light, about 5 minutes. Beat in the eggs one at a time, then beat in the egg white until smooth.

4. Scrape down and remove the beaters or paddle. Using a silicone spatula, fold in the flour mixture to make a stiff dough. Scrape it in lumps into the prepared pan, then press these together to make a uniform sheet of dough in the pan.

5. Sprinkle the coconut over the top and press it gently into the dough. Using the back of a flatware teaspoon, make about 80 thumb-print-sized indentations across the top of the cake. Put about a scant teaspoon of jam in each indentation.

6. Bake until the cake is browned and set and the jam has started to bubble, 23 to 25 minutes. Cool in the pan on a wire rack to room temperature, about 2 hours.

TESTER NOTE

The batter is super thick. You'll need to work to get it spread out. An offset spatula may not even do the trick. You can moisten your cleaned fingertips, press it out, and then continue to spread it with the spatula until it reaches the edges of the pan. Just make sure the top of the batter is, at most, damp, not wet.

CARROT CAKE WITH GOAT CHEESE BUTTERCREAM

There are two problems with most carrot cakes. One, they're dull because they're made with tasteless oils. And two, they're duller because they rely too much on the carrots for flavor. We've remedied the first problem by using a combo of butter and oil in the batter and the second by adding parsnips with the carrots. Parsnips lend the cake a surprisingly earthy finish, the better to match up with the supercreamy frosting, a dairy lover's holy grail.

For the cake

8 tablespoons (1 stick) cool unsalted butter, cut into small chunks, plus additional for the sheet pan

2¼ cups cake flour, plus additional for the sheet pan

2 teaspoons baking powder

1 teaspoon ground cinnamon

½ teaspoon baking soda

½ teaspoon freshly grated nutmeg

½ teaspoon salt

1¼ cups packed dark brown sugar

⅔ cup granulated white sugar

⅔ cup canola or vegetable oil

5 large eggs

2 cups shredded carrots (about 12 ounces peeled medium carrots)

1½ cups shredded parsnips (about 10 ounces peeled medium parsnips)

2 teaspoons finely minced orange zest

½ teaspoon orange extract

½ teaspoon vanilla extract

1 cup coarsely chopped pecans (about 4½ ounces)

1. Position the rack in the center of the oven. Heat the oven to 350°F. Generously butter and lightly flour the inside of a 13 x 18-inch lipped sheet pan.

2. Whisk the flour, baking powder, cinnamon, baking soda, nutmeg, and salt in a medium bowl until uniform.

3. Using a handheld electric mixer or a stand mixer with the paddle attachment, beat the butter, both sugars, and the oil in a large bowl at medium speed until light and fluffy, about 5 minutes.

4. Scrape down the inside of the bowl, then beat in the eggs one at a time. Add the carrots, parsnips, orange zest, orange extract, and vanilla; beat until uniform.

5. Turn off the mixer, add the flour mixture, and beat at low speed just until there are no dry specks of flour. Scrape down and remove the beaters or paddle. Fold in the nuts with a silicone spatula. Using an offset spatula, spread the thick batter evenly into the prepared pan.

6. Bake until set and golden brown, and until a toothpick or cake tester inserted into the center of the cake comes out clean, about 25 minutes. Cool in the pan on a wire rack to room temperature, about 1½ hours.

For the buttercream

12 tablespoons (1½ sticks) unsalted butter, softened to room temperature
8 ounces full-fat cream cheese, softened to room temperature
4 ounces soft goat cheese, at room temperature
¼ cup packed light brown sugar
¼ cup full-fat sour cream
2 teaspoons vanilla extract
2 to 3 cups confectioners' sugar

1. Using a handheld mixer or a stand mixer with the whisk attachment, beat the butter, cream cheese, goat cheese, and brown sugar in a large bowl at medium speed until the sugar has dissolved, about 3 minutes. Beat in the sour cream and vanilla until smooth.

2. Turn off the mixer; add 2 cups of the confectioners' sugar. Beat at low speed until combined. Continue beating, adding more confectioners' sugar in ¼-cup increments until the frosting is spreadable and can hold its shape on the side of a spatula. Using an offset spatula, spread and smooth the frosting over the cooled cake.

SNICKERDOODLE CAKE WITH SPICED BUTTERCREAM

Ever wanted a big ol' cake that tastes like a snickerdoodle cookie? Neither had we. Then we came up with this concoction. It's a sturdy, slightly chewy cake (not at all like the texture of a cookie) that gets topped with a cinnamon-nutmeg buttercream. Don't be tempted to substitute butter for the shortening in the cake. You want a fairly neutral flavor palette, more like the cookies for which this cake is named.

For the cake

¾ cup solid vegetable shortening, plus additional for the sheet pan
3¾ cups all-purpose flour
1 tablespoon baking powder
½ teaspoon salt
3 cups granulated white sugar
3 large eggs, at room temperature
1½ cups whole or 2% milk
1 tablespoon vanilla extract

1. Position the rack in the center of the oven. Heat the oven to 350°F. Generously grease the inside of a 13 x 18-inch lipped sheet pan.

2. Whisk the flour, baking powder, and salt in a medium bowl until uniform.

3. Using a handheld electric mixer or a stand mixer with the paddle attachment, beat the sugar and shortening in a large bowl at medium speed until light and creamy, about 3 minutes.

4. Scrape down the inside of the bowl, then beat in the eggs one at a time. Turn off the mixer and pour the flour mixture evenly over the top of the batter.

5. Beat at low speed while slowly pouring in the milk and vanilla; continue beating just until all the flour has been moistened. Using an offset spatula, spread the thick batter evenly into the prepared pan.

6. Bake until lightly browned and set, and until a toothpick or cake tester inserted into the center of the cake comes out clean, 28 to 30 minutes. Cool in the pan on a wire rack to room temperature, about 1½ hours.

For the buttercream

3 to 4½ cups confectioners' sugar
16 tablespoons (2 sticks) unsalted butter, softened to room temperature
⅓ cup heavy cream
1 tablespoon vanilla extract
2 teaspoons ground cinnamon
⅛ to ¼ teaspoon freshly grated nutmeg
⅛ teaspoon salt

1. Using a handheld electric mixer or a stand mixer with the whisk attachment, beat 2¾ cups of the confectioners' sugar and the butter in a large bowl at low speed for 1 minute. Increase the speed to medium and continue beating until smooth and creamy.

2. Add the cream, vanilla, cinnamon, nutmeg, and salt; continue beating until smooth, adding more confectioners' sugar in ¼-cup increments until the frosting is spreadable and can hold its shape on the side of a spatula. Using an offset spatula, smooth and spread the frosting evenly over the cooled cake.

TESTER NOTES

You can omit the frosting entirely. Instead, mix ¼ cup granulated white sugar, 1½ teaspoons ground cinnamon, and ¼ teaspoon grated nutmeg in a small bowl. Sprinkle evenly over the cake batter just before baking.

BROWN SUGAR CAKE WITH PUMPKIN BUTTERCREAM

We decided to top this straightforward cake with an autumnal extravaganza, a frosting that's rich and flavorful, a great way to end a meal anytime between Columbus Day and Thanksgiving. The technique for the cake batter is a little different: you add the flour just at the end, then the melted butter to help incorporate that flour.

For the cake
12 tablespoons (1½ sticks) unsalted butter, melted and cooled, plus additional for the sheet pan
1½ cups cake flour, plus additional for the sheet pan
10 large eggs, at room temperature
1½ cups packed dark brown sugar
4½ teaspoons vanilla extract
½ teaspoon salt

1. Position the rack in the center of the oven. Heat the oven to 350°F. Generously butter and lightly flour the inside of a 13 x 18-inch lipped sheet pan.

2. Using a handheld electric mixer or a stand mixer with the whisk attachment, beat the eggs and brown sugar in a large bowl at medium speed until doubled in volume, about 8 minutes. Beat in the vanilla and salt.

3. Scrape down and remove the beaters or paddle. Also scrape down the inside of the bowl. Sprinkle the flour over the batter. Using a silicone spatula, fold in the flour in wide, slow, even strokes until there are no undissolved specks.

4. Add the melted butter; fold gently until uniform. Use an offset spatula to spread the batter evenly into the prepared pan.

5. Bake until firm and lightly browned, and until a toothpick or cake tester inserted into the center of the cake comes out clean, 16 to 18 minutes. Cool in the pan on a wire rack to room temperature, about 1½ hours.

For the buttercream
10 tablespoons (1¼ sticks) unsalted butter, softened to room temperature
10 ounces full-fat cream cheese, softened to room temperature
¼ cup canned solid pack pumpkin
1 tablespoon vanilla extract
½ teaspoon ground cinnamon
¼ teaspoon freshly grated nutmeg
¼ teaspoon salt
4 to 5 cups confectioners' sugar
Up to ½ cup unsalted pumpkin seeds (aka pepitas), for topping

1. Using a handheld electric mixer or a stand mixer with the whisk attachment, beat the butter and cream cheese in a large bowl at medium speed until smooth, about 2 minutes. Add the pumpkin, vanilla, cinnamon, nutmeg, and salt; beat until smooth, about 1 minute.

2. Turn off the mixer, add 4 cups of the confectioners' sugar, and beat at low speed until smooth. Continue beating at low speed, adding more confectioners' sugar in ¼-cup increments, until the frosting will hold its shape. Using an offset spatula, spread and smooth the frosting over the cooled cake. Garnish the top with pumpkin seeds before serving.

FRUIT & NUT
SHEET CAKES

These go further afield. Some, like our orange sheet cake with its marmalade-laced buttercream, are based on classic recipes, morphed big to serve crowds. Others, like our sheet cake made from dried figs and dates with a smooth coffee frosting, are admittedly pure whimsy.

About Confectioners' Sugar

Our frostings and American buttercreams will use varying amounts of confectioners' sugar based on both the day's ambient humidity and the butter's residual moisture content. There's no real way to guess the exact amount of confectioners' sugar in any of our frostings, so we've almost always offered the amount as a range. We tested one of these buttercreams three times and used 4¼ , 4 ⅔, or 5 cups of confectioners' sugar, depending on the batch.

Since the amount is not a very helpful marker, go by the stated visual cues. In general, look for a smooth, creamy frosting that's not stiff or gummy. It should definitely hold its shape on the side of a spatula tilted this way and that. Taste it, too. Nothing beats mouthfeel for getting the perfect consistency in a rich frosting.

Remember that it's always easy to add a little more confectioners' sugar. It's harder to fix the frosting after you've put in too much, once it's turned dry and pasty. In general, you can add a tablespoon of heavy cream or whole milk to thin it out but it will never reach the perfection that you'll get by initially adding dribs and drabs until you hit the right "spreadability" and silky texture.

Storing Sheet Cakes

Most of the cakes in this book will keep for two days at room temperature if they're 1) cooled completely, 2) sealed tightly in their pans with plastic wrap, and 3) *not frosted or glazed*. In fact, most can be frozen for up to four months before they're frosted or glazed, provided you wrap them up tightly and have a big enough chest freezer to hold one of these cakes. Or cut the cake into smaller sections and freeze these individually. We've done this countless times, thawing the pieces to take to book groups or committee meetings.

Almost all the cakes should be served the day they're frosted or glazed. Those with a whipped cream topping should be served almost immediately. Those with a frosting or buttercream can stay at room temperature for up to six hours, but then they need to go into the fridge. They'll taste best at room temperature, so plan on letting them sit out on the counter for at least 30 minutes before you serve them.

That said, those with a glaze are the most exacting. They can hold perfect at room temperature for only a couple of hours. Refrigerating can turn them gummy. Unless the recipe states that you must glaze the cake warm, you can always glaze it fifteen minutes or so before serving, enough time for the glaze to set before you cut into the cake.

We don't advise covering most of these cakes in the fridge because the frosting will get smushed. Some of it can even come up with the plastic wrap. We have occasionally resorted to sticking toothpicks in the cakes to tent the plastic wrap over them. It's not a great solution and inevitably we've ended up with dented frosting.

About Nuts

Many of these cakes use a lot of nuts, between 1½ and 3½ cups' worth. Buying nuts can try even the most generous budget. Look for bulk bins at larger supermarkets, rather than the smaller, individual packets in the baking aisle. Or search out online retailers who offer good bargains on larger quantities. We've found that the Texas Pecan Company in Dallas, Texas, has particularly good prices on all sorts of nuts (www.texaspecanco.com). Store the shelled nuts in a sealed plastic bag or a sealed container in the freezer for up to one year. Don't worry about defrosting them. They'll thaw quickly as they're used in any recipe.

And One More Thing . . .

Remember that no amount of cream cheese or butter can cover the taste of inferior ingredients, of rancid nuts or cheap, thin marmalade. Buy the best you can comfortably afford. You're undoubtedly making these large-format desserts for a crowd. Put your best foot forward.

BLUEBERRY BUCKLE

A buckle is a New England tradition, a sturdy, somewhat dry batter, sort of like a quick bread's, often stocked with lots of berries, particularly blueberries, or sometimes chopped stone fruit. It's a deep-dish affair most of the time, but we've modified the ratios to make it a thinner sheet cake. That means you get way more blueberries in every bite. There's no frosting here. The cake's the thing! But beware the batter: it's thick and stiff. You'll need to use elbow grease to get it spread into the pan.

20 tablespoons (2½ sticks) cool unsalted butter, cut into small chunks, plus additional for the sheet pan
5 cups all-purpose flour
2½ cups plus 2 tablespoons granulated white sugar
2 teaspoons ground cinnamon
1¼ teaspoons salt
At least 2 tablespoons cold heavy cream
4½ teaspoons baking powder
2 large eggs plus 1 large egg white, at room temperature
1¼ cups whole or 2% milk
1 tablespoon vanilla extract
1¼ pounds fresh blueberries (about 4 cups) or 1 pound frozen blueberries (do not thaw)
Confectioners' sugar, for topping

1. Position the rack in the center of the oven. Heat the oven to 350°F. Generously butter the inside of a 13 x 18-inch lipped sheet pan.

2. Put 1¼ cups of the flour, ¾ cup of the white sugar, the cinnamon, and ¼ teaspoon of the salt in a large food processor. Cover and pulse to combine.

3. Add 10 tablespoons of the butter. Cover and pulse until a coarse, gritty powder. Add 2 tablespoons cream, cover, and pulse to form a crumbly amalgam that will hold its shape when squeezed. Add more cream in 1-teaspoon increments to get the right consistency.

4. Whisk the remaining 3¾ cups flour, the remaining 1 teaspoon salt, and the baking powder in a medium bowl until uniform.

5. Using a handheld electric mixer or a stand mixer with the paddle attachment, beat the remaining 1¾ cups plus 2 tablespoons white sugar with the remaining 10 tablespoons butter in a large bowl at medium speed until creamy, light, and fluffy, about 6 minutes.

6. Scrape down the inside of the bowl. Beat in the eggs one at a time, followed by the egg white, until smooth. Stop the mixer and pour the flour and baking powder mixture on top of the batter. Beating at low speed, add the milk and vanilla in a slow stream; continue beating just until all the flour has been moistened.

7. Using an offset spatula, spread the very thick batter evenly into the prepared pan. Sprinkle the blueberries evenly over the top. Squeeze and scatter the topping from the food processor over the cake, creating grainy bits, little pebbles, and a generally irregular surface.

8. Bake until lightly browned, and until a toothpick or cake tester inserted into the center of the cake without hitting a blueberry comes out clean, about 40 minutes. Cool in the pan on a wire rack for at least 20 minutes before cutting into squares. Dust with confectioners' sugar before serving, if desired.

TESTER NOTES

The blueberries aren't folded in; they're scattered on top. The cake will rise and engulf them as it bakes so they don't all end up on the bottom. If you use frozen blueberries, increase the baking time by as much as ten minutes and cover the buckle with aluminum foil if it browns too deeply before it is set.

STRAWBERRY SHORTCAKE

There are two types of shortcake lovers: those who like dense, thick, chewy shortcakes and those who are right. Our shortcake is quite airy, not springy like a sponge cake, but a bit sturdier without losing its delicate texture. You can cut it out in squares to serve in bowls under the whipped cream and berries. Or you can use a cookie cutter to make fancier shapes. Or you can cut out small rounds and make little layer cakes with plenty of whipped cream in the stacks. If you want to get all grandmotherly, skip the fresh berries, thaw frozen sliced strawberries, and spoon the soupy stuff over the whipped cream.

For the cake
24 tablespoons (3 sticks) cool unsalted butter, cut into small chunks, plus additional for the sheet pan
6 cups all-purpose flour
4½ teaspoons baking powder
6 large eggs (3 whole and 3 separated), plus 3 large egg whites, at room temperature
½ teaspoon salt
2¾ cups granulated white sugar
½ cup plus 1 tablespoon solid vegetable shortening
4½ teaspoons vanilla extract

1. Position the rack in the center of the oven. Heat the oven to 350°F. Generously butter the inside of a 13 x 18-inch lipped sheet pan.

2. Whisk the flour and baking powder in a medium bowl until uniform.

3. Using a handheld mixer or a stand mixer with the whisk attachment, beat the six egg whites and salt in a large bowl at low speed until foamy. Increase the speed to high and beat until you can make droopy peaks. Beating at high speed, drizzle in ¾ cup of the sugar. Continue beating until you can make firm peaks.

4. Using a handheld electric mixer with clean, dry beaters or a stand mixer with the paddle attachment, beat the butter, shortening, and the remaining 2 cups sugar in a second large bowl at medium speed until light and fluffy, about 6 minutes. Scrape down the inside of the bowl, then beat in the three whole eggs one at a time, followed by the three egg yolks one at a time. Beat in the vanilla until smooth and uniform.

5. Turn off the mixer, add the flour mixture, and beat at low speed just until incorporated. Add half the beaten egg white mixture; beat at low speed to form a thick, stiff batter, no more than 1 minute.

6. Turn off the mixer; scrape down and remove the beaters or paddle. Fold in the remainder of the egg white mixture with a silicone spatula, using wide, gentle arcs. There may be a few white streaks visible. Use an offset spatula to spread this batter into the prepared pan.

7. Bake until firm to the touch, and until a toothpick or cake tester inserted into the center of the cake comes out clean, about 25 minutes. Cool in the pan on a wire rack until room temperature, about 2 hours.

For the sweetened whipped cream
3 cups cold heavy cream
½ cup confectioners' sugar
1 tablespoon vanilla extract

For the topping
2½ pounds fresh strawberries, hulled and quartered (about 6 cups)

1. Using a handheld electric mixer or a stand mixer with the whisk attachment, beat the cream, confectioners' sugar, and vanilla in a large bowl at high speed just until it holds a soft shape on a silicone spatula.

2. Spoon and spread the whipped cream evenly over the cooled cake. Lay the quartered strawberries across the top of the cake before serving.

TESTER NOTES
For the most luxurious whipped cream, chill the mixer beaters or whisk as well as the bowl for at least twenty minutes or even overnight before whipping the cream. Because the confectioners' sugar will keep the whipped cream from deflating too quickly, you can put it on the cake up to three hours in advance. Lightly cover the whole thing with plastic wrap and store it in the fridge.

APPLE CAKE WITH TOASTED WALNUTS

No doubt about it: toasted walnut oil will make the cake taste fantastic. But also no doubt about it: toasted walnut oil is pricey. What's more, it can go bad quickly. Check out online suppliers for good prices. Open the can or jar, rub a little of the oil in your palm, and smell it to make sure it's not rancid. If so, send it back for a full refund— or take it back to the store! And after the can or jar is opened, store it in the fridge for about a month, using it to make scrambled eggs divine or to drizzle over chopped vegetable salads.

For the cake

7 large tart apples, such as Granny Smith or Empire, peeled, cored, and chopped
1¾ cups plus 1 tablespoon granulated white sugar
¾ cup toasted walnut oil, plus additional for the sheet pan
3⅔ cups all-purpose flour
1¼ teaspoons baking powder
1 teaspoon ground cinnamon
½ teaspoon baking soda
½ teaspoon salt
2 large eggs plus 1 large egg white, at room temperature
2 teaspoons vanilla extract
3 cups walnut pieces

1. Stir the apples and sugar in a large bowl until well coated. Set aside at room temperature for 30 minutes to macerate, stirring occasionally.

2. Position the rack in the center of the oven. Heat the oven to 350°F. Generously oil the inside of a 13 x 18-inch lipped sheet pan.

3. Whisk the flour, baking powder, cinnamon, baking soda, and salt in a medium bowl until uniform.

4. Using a wooden spoon, stir the eggs, egg white, and vanilla into the apple mixture until smooth, then stir in the walnut oil until well combined.

5. Add the flour mixture and stir just until there are no dry bits of flour. The batter will be very thick. Using an offset spatula, spread the batter evenly into the prepared pan.

6. Bake until lightly browned and set and a toothpick or cake tester inserted into the center of the cake comes out clean, 23 to 25 minutes. Maintain the oven's temperature. Cool in the pan on a wire rack until room temperature, about 1½ hours.

7. As the cake cools, spread the walnut pieces on a second large lipped sheet pan. Bake until fragrant and lightly browned, stirring occasionally, about 6 minutes. Cool in the pan to room temperature, about 1 hour.

For the glaze

9 tablespoons water
3 tablespoons light corn syrup
1 tablespoon vanilla extract
4 to 5 cups confectioners' sugar

1. Mix the water and corn syrup in a large saucepan and bring to a boil over medium-high heat, stirring occasionally. Boil for 1 minute. Remove from the heat and stir in the vanilla.

2. Stir in 3½ cups of the confectioners' sugar until smooth. Then continue adding more confectioners' sugar in ¼-cup increments until the glaze is spreadable but not as thick as a standard frosting, like a cross between a drizzle and a frosting.

3. Drizzle and spread this mixture over the cake while still hot. Sprinkle the toasted walnuts over the top and press down gently with the back of a wooden spoon so they adhere.

TESTER NOTES

The apples will continue to macerate in the sugar even after baking, leading to a gummy cake by the next day. You'll just need to eat this one up the day you make it!

LEMONADE CAKE WITH LEMON CURD WHIPPED CREAM

We feel the best lemon cakes are made with lemonade, a concentrated jolt of flavor that gives the cake a particularly summery stripe (even in winter). Make sure you use regular lemonade concentrate, not low-sugar or sugar-free. The frosting here is simple but gorgeously sophisticated: lemon curd folded into whipped cream. (See the Tester Note below for a shortcut.)

For the lemon curd

2 teaspoons finely grated lemon zest plus ½ cup fresh lemon juice
½ cup granulated white sugar
3 large eggs, at room temperature
6 tablespoons (¾ stick) unsalted butter, cut into small bits

1. Set up a double boiler or a heat-safe bowl that fits snugly over a medium saucepan with about 1 inch of slowly simmering water. Whisk the lemon juice and sugar in the top half of the double boiler or the bowl for a few seconds, then whisk in the eggs, butter, and lemon zest. Continue whisking—do not stop—until thick and rich, about 12 minutes. Scrape into a medium bowl and refrigerate for at least 4 hours or overnight.

For the cake

9 tablespoons (1 stick plus 1 tablespoon) cool unsalted butter, cut into chunks, plus additional for the sheet pan

3 cups cake flour, plus additional for the sheet
    pan
½ teaspoon baking soda
½ teaspoon salt
1½ cups granulated white sugar
1 tablespoon finely grated lemon zest
3 large eggs plus 3 large egg whites, at room
    temperature
5 tablespoons frozen lemonade concentrate,
    thawed
2 teaspoons vanilla extract
2 teaspoons lemon extract

1. Position the rack in the center of the oven.
Heat the oven to 350°F. Generously butter and
lightly flour the inside of a 13 x 18-inch lipped
sheet pan. Whisk the flour, baking soda, and
salt in a medium bowl until uniform.

2. Using a handheld electric mixer or a stand
mixer with the paddle attachment, beat the
sugar, butter, and lemon zest in a large bowl at
medium speed until creamy, light, and fluffy,
about 5 minutes. Scrape down the inside of the
bowl, then beat in the eggs one at a time,
followed by the egg whites one at a time.

3. Beat in the lemonade concentrate, vanilla,
and lemon extract until smooth. Turn off the
mixer; pour the flour mixture over the top of
the batter. Beat at medium speed to create a
very thick batter. Using an offset spatula,
spread the somewhat stiff batter evenly into the
prepared pan.

4. Bake until pale beige and set, and until a
toothpick or cake tester inserted into the center
of the cake comes out clean, 18 to 20 minutes.
Cool in the pan on a wire rack to room temperature, about 1½ hours.

For the whipped cream
1½ cups heavy cream
¾ cup confectioners' sugar
¼ teaspoon salt
Lemon curd (see pg 62)

1. Using a handheld electric mixer or a stand
mixer with the whisk attachment, beat the
cream, confectioners' sugar, and salt in a large
bowl at high speed until you can make soft
peaks. Scrape down and remove the beaters or
whisk.

2. Using a silicone spatula, fold in the lemon
curd until uniform. Use that same spatula to
spoon and spread the whipped cream mixture
evenly over the cooled cake.

TESTER NOTES
You can substitute purchased lemon curd for the
homemade. Skip step 1 and use 2 cups (about two
10-ounce jars). If possible, use a bottled lemon curd
that includes lots of real butter for the best flavor.
Notice, too, that this whipped cream is sweeter than
the one used for the Strawberry Shortcake (page
58). Here, we want a bigger contrast to the tart
lemon flavor.

ORANGE CAKE WITH MARMALADE BUTTERCREAM

This may be the second-best birthday cake in the bunch (after the plain cake with confetti frosting on page 35). This one's pretty sturdy to sit under a thick, cream cheese–laced buttercream. It'll sure hold lots of candles! It'll also go well with vanilla or chocolate ice cream—or even lemon sorbet.

For the cake

20 tablespoons (2½ sticks) cool unsalted butter, cut into small chunks, plus additional for the sheet pan
2½ cups all-purpose flour
2 teaspoons baking powder
1 teaspoon salt
1 cup granulated white sugar
1 tablespoon finely grated orange zest plus ⅔ cup fresh orange juice
1 tablespoon finely grated lemon zest
5 large eggs plus 1 large egg white, at room temperature
⅔ cup orange marmalade

1. Position the rack in the center of the oven. Heat the oven to 350°F. Generously butter the inside of a 13 x 18-inch lipped sheet pan.

2. Whisk the flour, baking powder, and salt in a medium bowl until uniform.

3. Using a handheld electric mixer or a stand mixer with the paddle attachment, beat the butter, sugar, and both zests in a large bowl until light and creamy, about 6 minutes. Beat in the eggs one at a time, then beat in the egg white.

4. Scrape down the inside of the bowl, then beat in the marmalade. Turn off the mixer and pour the flour mixture evenly on top of the batter. Beat at low speed while slowly pouring in the orange juice, until there are no bits of dry flour in the batter. Using an offset spatula, spread the batter into the prepared pan.

5. Bake until puffed and set, and until a toothpick or a cake tester inserted into the center of the cake comes out clean, about 20 minutes. Cool in the pan on a wire rack until room temperature, about 1½ hours

For the buttercream

16 tablespoons (2 sticks) unsalted butter, softened to room temperature
8 ounces full-fat cream cheese, at room temperature
⅔ cup orange marmalade
¼ cup heavy cream
½ teaspoon vanilla extract
3 to 4 cups confectioners' sugar

1. Using a handheld electric mixer or a stand mixer with the whisk attachment, beat the butter and cream cheese in a large bowl at medium speed until smooth, about 1 minute. Add the marmalade, cream, and vanilla; continue beating until creamy, about 1 more minute.

2. Turn off the mixer, add 2 cups of the confectioners' sugar, and beat at low speed until combined. Increase the speed to medium and beat, adding more confectioners' sugar in ¼-cup increments, until the frosting is spreadable but can still hold its shape on the side of a spatula. Using an offset spatula, spread and smooth the frosting evenly over the cooled cake.

PINEAPPLE CAKE WITH BANANA BUTTERCREAM

You'll need to get a pantry staple from your mom's day to make this cake: canned crushed pineapple in heavy syrup. That syrup will provide lots of flavor as well as much of the sugar for the batter. It'll yield a surprisingly dense cake that freezes (unfrosted) beautifully. And about that frosting? Like others in this book, it's actually a modified American buttercream with cream cheese in the mix for an added depth of flavor against the bananas. Make sure they're quite ripe, with lots of brown (and maybe a few black) spots on their skins.

For the cake
12½ tablespoons (1 stick plus 4½ tablespoons) cool unsalted butter, cut into small chunks, plus additional for the sheet pan

4 cups cake flour, plus additional for the sheet pan

2½ teaspoons baking powder

½ teaspoon baking soda

4 large eggs, separated, plus 1 large egg white, at room temperature

½ teaspoon salt

1 cup plus 3 tablespoons granulated white sugar

One 20-ounce can pineapple chunks in heavy syrup, drained with the syrup reserved

2 teaspoons vanilla extract

2 tablespoons whole or 2% milk

1. Position the rack in the center of the oven. Heat the oven to 350°F. Generously butter and lightly flour the inside of a 13 x 18-inch lipped sheet pan.

2. Whisk the cake flour, baking powder, and baking soda in a medium bowl until uniform.

3. Using a handheld electric mixer or a stand mixer with the whisk attachment, beat the five egg whites and salt in a large bowl at low speed until foamy. Then increase the speed to high and continue beating until you can make droopy peaks.

4. Using a handheld mixer with clean, dry beaters or a stand mixer with the paddle attachment, beat the butter and sugar in a second large bowl at medium speed until light and fluffy, about 5 minutes.

5. Scrape down the inside of the bowl, then beat in the four egg yolks one at a time. Beat in the drained pineapple and vanilla until uniform.

6. Turn off the mixer; pour the flour mixture over the batter. Beating at medium speed, add the milk in a steady stream, then the reserved pineapple syrup. Continue beating just until there are no dry specks of flour in the batter. Scrape down and remove the beaters or paddle.

7. Using a silicone spatula, fold in half the beaten egg whites until uniform and smooth. Add the remaining egg whites and fold gently, smoothly, and slowly, just until mixed throughout but not deflated very much. There will be some white streaks visible. Use that spatula to pour and spread the batter into the prepared pan.

8. Bake until firm and set, and until a toothpick or cake tester inserted into the center of the cake comes out clean, 18 to 20 minutes. Cool in the pan on a wire rack to room temperature, about 1½ hours.

For the buttercream

12 tablespoons (1½ sticks) unsalted butter, softened to room temperature
4 ounces full-fat or low-fat cream cheese, softened to room temperature
2 very ripe medium bananas, peeled and cut into chunks
2 tablespoons banana liqueur, such as crème de banane
1 teaspoon vanilla extract
6 to 8 cups confectioners' sugar

1. Using a handheld electric mixer with clean, dry beaters or the stand mixer with a clean, dry whisk attachment, beat the butter and cream cheese in a clean, dry large bowl until smooth and light, about 2 minutes. Beat in the banana chunks and liqueur until smooth.

2. Turn off the mixer, add 6 cups of the confectioners' sugar, and beat at low speed until smooth. Continue beating at low speed, adding more confectioners' sugar in ⅓-cup increments, until the batter will mound on the side of a spatula. Using an offset spatula, spread and smooth the frosting evenly over the cooled cake.

TESTER NOTES
Because the canned pineapple bits will fall through a standard colander, drain the canned pineapple bits in a fine-mesh sieve or in a standard colander lined with cheesecloth or even paper towels.

COCONUT CAKE WITH WHITE CHOCOLATE BUTTERCREAM

If you're from the South, you'll expect a seven-minute frosting on a coconut sheet cake. Sure, it's the standard, but we wanted to take our coconut concoction over the top; so we crafted a frosting that's got lots of white chocolate in the buttery mix. Don't worry: there's coconut in there, too. All in all, this one's a coconut lover's paradise.

For the cake

24 tablespoons (3 sticks) cool unsalted butter, cut into small chunks, plus additional for the sheet pan
3 cups all-purpose flour, plus additional for the sheet pan
1 teaspoon baking powder
½ teaspoon baking soda
½ teaspoon salt
2 cups granulated white sugar
5 large eggs, at room temperature
1½ teaspoons vanilla extract
1½ teaspoons almond extract
1 cup whole or 2% milk
One 7-ounce package sweetened shredded coconut (about 2 cups)

1. Position the rack in the center of the oven. Heat the oven to 350°F. Generously butter and lightly flour the inside of a 13 x 18-inch lipped sheet pan.

2. Whisk the flour, baking powder, baking soda, and salt in a medium bowl until uniform.

3. Using a handheld electric mixer or a stand mixer with the paddle attachment, beat the sugar and butter in a large bowl at medium speed until light and fluffy, about 6 minutes.

4. Scrape down the inside of the bowl, then beat in the eggs one at a time. Beat in the vanilla and almond extracts until smooth and uniform.

5. Turn off the mixer, scrape down the bowl again, and pour the flour mixture on top of the batter. Beat at medium speed while slowly pouring in the milk; continue beating just until there are no bits of dry flour in the batter. Beat in the coconut until uniform. Using an offset spatula, spread the batter evenly into the prepared pan.

6. Bake until lightly browned and set to the touch, and until a toothpick or cake tester inserted into the center of the cake comes out clean, 25 to 28 minutes. Cool in the pan on a wire rack to room temperature, about 2 hours. Maintain the oven's temperature.

For the buttercream

2 cups unsweetened shredded coconut
6 ounces chopped white chocolate or white chocolate chips
2 tablespoons heavy cream
16 tablespoons (2 sticks) unsalted butter, softened to room temperature
3 to 4 cups confectioners' sugar
1 tablespoon vanilla extract
½ teaspoon almond extract

1. As the cake cools, spread the coconut on a large lipped sheet pan. Toast in the oven until lightly browned, stirring occasionally, about 10 minutes. Set aside to cool to room temperature, about 1 hour.

2. Put the white chocolate and cream in a small saucepan set over low heat. Heat, stirring almost the whole time, until about three-quarters of the chocolate has melted. Remove from the heat and continue stirring until smooth. Set aside to cool for 20 minutes.

3. Using a handheld electric mixer or a stand mixer with the whisk attachment, beat the butter and 2½ cups of the confectioners' sugar in a large bowl at medium speed until smooth.

4. Beat in the white chocolate mixture, then the vanilla and almond extracts until smooth. Continue beating at low speed, adding more confectioners' sugar in ¼-cup increments, until the frosting is thick and can mound on the side of a spatula. Using an offset spatula, spread and smooth the frosting over the cooled cake. Sprinkle the toasted coconut on top.

BANANA CAKE WITH COCOA BUTTERCREAM

If you're not a fan of banana bread, pass on this recipe. But if you like the stuff as much as we do, you'll want to try this coffee cake–like sheet cake, a treat so long as the bananas are plenty ripe with brown (or even a few black) spots on their skins. The frosting is super thick, even a little sticky, the better to pair with that classic, chewy, banana-bread texture.

For the cake

¾ cup plus 1 tablespoon solid vegetable shortening, plus additional for the sheet pan

2⅔ cups cake flour, plus additional for the sheet pan

1½ teaspoons baking powder

½ teaspoon baking soda

½ teaspoon salt

4 very ripe medium bananas (lots of dark spots), peeled and cut into chunks

1 cup packed light brown sugar

⅓ cup granulated white sugar

4 large eggs, at room temperature

1 tablespoon vanilla extract

⅔ cup whole or 2% milk

1. Position the rack in the center of the oven. Heat the oven to 350°F. Generously grease and lightly flour the inside of a 13 x 18-inch lipped sheet pan.

2. Whisk the flour, baking powder, baking soda, and salt in a medium bowl until uniform.

3. Mash the bananas to a paste in a small bowl with a flatware fork or a potato masher.

4. Using a handheld electric mixer or a stand mixer with the whisk attachment, beat the shortening, brown sugar, and white sugar at medium speed in a large bowl until creamy and light, about 4 minutes.

5. Scrape down the inside of the bowl, then beat in the eggs one a time. Add the mashed bananas and vanilla; beat at low speed until combined. The batter may look broken at this stage.

6. Turn off the mixer and pour the flour mixture evenly on top of the batter. Beat at low speed while slowly pouring in the milk; continue beating just until there are no bits of dry flour in the batter. Using an offset spatula, spread the batter evenly into the prepared pan.

7. Bake until set to the touch and a toothpick or cake tester inserted into the center of the cake comes out clean, 18 to 20 minutes. Cool in the pan on a wire rack to room temperature, about 2 hours.

For the buttercream

16 tablespoons (2 sticks) unsalted butter, softened to room temperature
8 ounces full-fat cream cheese, softened to room temperature
2 tablespoons dark corn syrup
2 tablespoons heavy cream
1 tablespoon vanilla extract
⅔ cup unsweetened cocoa powder
¼ teaspoon salt
3 to 4 cups confectioners' sugar

1. Using a handheld electric mixer or a stand mixer with the whisk attachment, beat the butter and cream cheese in a large bowl at medium speed until smooth and luscious, about 2 minutes. Beat in the corn syrup, cream, and vanilla until smooth.

2. Turn off the mixer; add the cocoa powder and salt. Beat at low speed until uniform. Turn off the mixer again and add 2½ cups of the confectioners' sugar. Beat at low speed until combined, then increase the speed a bit and beat, adding more confectioners' sugar in ¼-cup increments, until the frosting is spreadable and can hold its shape on the side of a spatula. Using an offset spatula, spread and smooth the frosting evenly over the cooled cake.

TESTER NOTES
We used shortening in this cake, rather than butter, because the neutral flavor of the shortening lets the taste of the bananas come through unimpeded.

FIG AND DATE CAKE WITH COFFEE BUTTERCREAM

Without a doubt, this one's the densest sheet cake in the book. It's sort of a cross between an Old World fruitcake and a modern coffee cake. Use only baking dates, those sugared (or dextrose-coated) chopped date bits that come in small boxes in the baking aisle of almost all North American supermarkets. Fresher dates will be too sticky to make a successful batter. The whole thing needs a strong cup of coffee. We gave it one in the form of this rich buttercream!

For the cake

2 cups water
1 teaspoon baking soda
8 ounces chopped pitted baking dates
8 ounces dried figs, stemmed and quartered
½ cup bourbon
2 teaspoons vanilla extract
1 cup canola or vegetable oil, plus additional for the sheet pan
3 cups cake flour
2 teaspoons baking powder
1 teaspoon ground cinnamon
½ teaspoon freshly grated nutmeg
½ teaspoon salt
2 cups packed light brown sugar
3 large eggs, at room temperature
2 cups sliced almonds

1. Stir the water and baking soda in a large saucepan until the soda dissolves. Mix in the baking dates and quartered figs. Bring to a simmer over medium-high heat, stirring often. Cover and set aside off the heat for 20 minutes.

2. Pour the dried fruit mixture into a large blender or a food processor; add the bourbon and vanilla. Cover and blend or process until fairly smooth. Set aside to cool to room temperature, about 1 hour.

3. Position the rack in the center of the oven. Heat the oven to 350°F. Generously oil the inside of a 13 x 18-inch lipped sheet pan.

4. Whisk the flour, baking powder, cinnamon, nutmeg, and salt in a medium bowl until uniform.

5. Using a handheld electric mixer or a stand mixer with the whisk attachment, beat the brown sugar and eggs in a large bowl at medium speed until you can make wide ribbons, about 6 minutes. Beat in the oil until smooth.

6. Pour and scrape the date-fig mixture into the bowl; beat at low speed until smooth. Beat in the almonds; then turn off the mixer, add the flour mixture, and beat at low speed to form a thick batter. Using an offset spatula, spread the very thick batter into the prepared pan.

7. Bake until puffed and set, and until a toothpick inserted into the center of the cake comes out clean, 30 to 35 minutes. Cool in the pan on a wire rack until room temperature, about 2 hours.

For the buttercream

8 ounces full-fat cream cheese, softened to
    room temperature
16 tablespoons (2 sticks) unsalted butter,
    softened to room temperature
¼ cup light corn syrup
4½ teaspoons instant coffee powder
3 to 4 cups confectioners' sugar
Dark roasted coffee beans, for topping

1. Using a handheld electric mixer or a stand
mixer with the whisk attachment, beat the
cream cheese and butter in a large bowl at
medium speed until smooth and even light,
about 3 minutes. Beat in the corn syrup and
instant coffee powder until uniform.

2. Turn off the mixer, add 2½ cups of the
confectioners' sugar, and beat at low speed until
combined. Scrape down the inside of the bowl
and beat in ½ cup confectioners' sugar.

3. Continue beating in more confectioners'
sugar in ¼-cup increments until the batter is
thick and will mound on the side of a spatula.
Using an offset spatula, spread and smooth the
frosting evenly over the cooled cake. Sprinkle
the coffee beans on top.

TESTER NOTES

For an even bigger pop of flavor, substitute instant
espresso powder for the instant coffee in the frosting.

GLUTEN-FREE LEMON BUTTERMILK CAKE WITH CARAMEL GLAZE

*Try this: a bright lemony cake, tender and light,
with a hot caramel sauce poured on top. This
wheat-free cake has a delicate crumb, just a
little smoother than a pound cake. If you don't
tell people it's gluten-free, they may not know.
Because of the oats and buckwheat flour, the
cake is best served in its first twenty-four hours. It
becomes a little gummy if it sits around too long.
Unfortunately, it also doesn't freeze very well.
You'll just have to eat it up!*

For the cake

16 tablespoons (2 sticks) unsalted butter, melted
    and cooled to room temperature, plus
    additional for the sheet pan
1 cup certified gluten-free yellow cornmeal
1 cup buckwheat flour
1 cup certified gluten-free rolled oats
½ cup cornstarch
½ cup white rice flour
2 teaspoons baking powder
1 teaspoon baking soda
½ teaspoon salt
2 cups granulated white sugar
4 large eggs, at room temperature
1⅓ cups regular cultured buttermilk
¼ cup fresh lemon juice
2 teaspoons vanilla extract

1. Position the rack in the center of the oven.
Heat the oven to 350°F. Generously butter the
inside of a 13 x 18-inch lipped sheet pan.

2. Whisk the cornmeal, buckwheat flour, oats,
cornstarch, rice flour, baking powder, baking
soda, and salt in a medium bowl until uniform.

3. Using a handheld electric mixer or a stand mixer with the paddle attachment, beat the sugar and eggs in a large bowl until you can make wide ribbons, about 5 minutes.

4. Beat in the melted butter until smooth. Turn off the mixer; pour the cornmeal mixture evenly on top of the batter. Beat at low speed while slowly pouring in the buttermilk, lemon juice, and vanilla; continue beating until smooth. Use an offset spatula to spread and smooth the batter evenly into the prepared pan.

5. Bake until lightly browned, and until a toothpick or cake tester inserted into the center of the cake comes out clean, about 20 minutes. Cool in the pan on a wire rack to room temperature, about 1½ hours.

For the glaze

1 cup packed light brown sugar
8 tablespoons (1 stick) unsalted butter, cut into small pieces
½ cup heavy cream
1 teaspoon fresh lemon juice
1 teaspoon vanilla extract
½ teaspoon salt

1. Stir the brown sugar, butter, cream, lemon juice, vanilla, and salt in a large skillet set over medium heat until the sugar dissolves. Reduce the heat to low and continue cooking, stirring frequently, until the mixture comes to a boil. Boil for 3 minutes.

2. Set the skillet off the heat and cool until thickened but still pourable, stirring occasionally, 10 to 15 minutes. Pour over the cake and spread smooth with an offset spatula.

TESTER NOTES

Oats and buckwheat are indeed gluten-free—provided they have been processed or milled in a certified gluten-free facility. The problem with both is that they are often handled in facilities that also process wheat. It's nigh unto impossible to get rid of its dust. Search out grains processed in certified facilities, if this matters to you or yours. In North America, baking powder is almost always cut with cornstarch as a drying agent; in the United Kingdom, however, it can use a wheat-based additive. Check the manufacturer's websites if you're in doubt.

LEMON RICOTTA CAKE WITH SWEETENED WHIPPED CREAM AND BERRIES

Because there's not much flour in this batter, the crumb is chewy, sort of like a cross between a custard pie and a buttery cake. The cake is very thin but a good platform for the whipped cream and berries. If you really want to go old school, omit the berries and use 1½ pounds of frozen mixed berries, thawed and drained. Spoon these soupy, soft berry bits over each slice of cake and whipped cream.

30 tablespoons (3¾ sticks) unsalted butter, plus additional for the sheet pan
1¾ cups plus 2 tablespoons granulated white sugar
7 large eggs, separated, at room temperature
2½ cups whole-milk ricotta
2 teaspoons vanilla extract
Up to 2 teaspoons lemon extract
½ cup plus 1 tablespoon all-purpose flour
1 tablespoon baking powder
½ teaspoon salt
Sweetened Whipped Cream (see page 59)
12 ounces fresh blackberries (about 2 cups), for topping
8 ounces fresh raspberries (about 2 cups), for topping

1. Position the rack in the center of the oven. Heat the oven to 325°F. Generously butter the inside of a 13 x 18-inch lipped sheet pan.

2. Using a handheld electric beater or a stand mixer with the paddle attachment, beat the butter and sugar in a large bowl at medium speed until soft, smooth, and velvety, about 5 minutes.

3. Scrape down the inside of the bowl, then beat in the egg yolks one at a time. Beat in the ricotta, vanilla, and lemon extract until uniform and smooth. Add the flour and baking powder. Beat at low speed just until incorporated, no more than a few seconds.

4. Using a handheld mixer with clean, dry beaters or a stand mixer with the whisk attachment, beat the egg whites and salt in a second large bowl at low speed until foamy, then at high speed until you can make soft peaks.

5. Use a silicone spatula to fold the beaten egg whites into the batter, using gentle, smooth arcs to keep as much loft in the whites as possible. Scrape and spread the batter into the prepared pan.

6. Bake until somewhat puffed, lightly browned at the edges and set, about 30 minutes. Cool in the pan on a wire rack to room temperature, about 2 hours.

7. Slice the cake into squares or rectangles and transfer these to serving plates or a platter. Dollop each serving with the whipped cream and top with berries.

PECAN CAKE WITH CARAMEL-COCONUT FROSTING

This cake is fashioned on those infamous Girl Scout cookies. No, not the minty ones. The other ones that recently had a name change. We're not saying. We don't want to get sued. (We don't even want to tell you about the run-in we once had with the creamy-orange-and-vanilla-ice-pop people.) Here, you get an intense, pecan-laced cake with a rich cooked coconut frosting that's then drizzled with chocolate sauce. You know the cookies. Wait until you taste the cake.

For the cake

18 tablespoons (2 sticks plus 2 tablespoons) cool unsalted butter, cut into small chunks, plus additional for the sheet pan
1½ cups chopped pecans
3 cups cake flour, plus additional for the sheet pan
2 teaspoons baking powder
½ teaspoon salt
2 cups granulated white sugar
4 large eggs, at room temperature
2 teaspoons vanilla extract
1 cup whole or 2% milk

1. Melt 2 tablespoons of the butter in a large skillet set over medium-low heat. Add the chopped pecans and cook, stirring often, until lightly browned and aromatic, about 3 minutes. Set aside to cool to room temperature, about 30 minutes.

2. Position the rack in the center of the oven. Heat the oven to 350°F. Generously butter and lightly flour the inside of a 13 x 18-inch lipped sheet pan.

3. Whisk the flour, baking powder, and salt in a medium bowl until uniform.

4. Using a handheld electric mixer or a stand mixer with the paddle attachment, beat the remaining 16 tablespoons (2 sticks) butter and the sugar in a large bowl at medium speed until creamy, light, and even fluffy, about 4 minutes. Beat in the eggs one at a time, then beat in the vanilla until smooth.

5. Turn off the mixer; pour the flour mixture evenly on top of the batter. Beat at low speed while slowly pouring in the milk; continue beating until there are no bits of dry flour in the batter. Scrape down and remove the beaters or paddle.

6. Fold in the nut mixture with a silicone spatula until uniform throughout the batter. Using an offset spatula, spread the batter evenly into the prepared pan.

7. Bake until set to the touch, and until a toothpick inserted into the center of the cake comes out clean, about 25 minutes. Cool in the pan on a wire rack to room temperature, about 1½ hours.

For the frosting

4 large eggs, at room temperature

1½ cups granulated white sugar

10½ tablespoons (1 stick plus 2½ tablespoons) unsalted butter

½ cup evaporated whole milk

3 cups unsweetened shredded coconut

1 teaspoon vanilla extract

About ½ cup purchased chocolate sauce, for topping

1. Whisk the eggs in a large bowl until creamy and uniform.

2. Heat the sugar, butter, and evaporated milk in a large saucepan set over medium heat until the butter melts, stirring often. Clip a candy thermometer to the inside of the pan, reduce the heat to medium-low, and continue heating, stirring occasionally, until the mixture's temperature reaches 230°F (the thread stage on some candy thermometers).

3. Whisk about half the hot sugar mixture into the beaten eggs in a steady stream until uniform. Then whisk this combined mixture into the remaining sugar mixture until smooth.

4. Set the pan back over medium heat and cook, whisking all the while, until boiling. Boil and whisk for 2 minutes. Whisk in the coconut and vanilla. Cool for 15 to 20 minutes, whisking occasionally.

5. Spread and smooth the cooked frosting over the cooled cake. Drizzle the chocolate sauce over the top, either making long diagonal lines across the cake or splattering the sauce for a messier effect.

MACAROON CAKE WITH RASPBERRY BUTTERCREAM

Consider this our sheet cake tribute to the Linzer tart, which is raspberry jam spread onto almond pastry. Here, the almond cake is a little bit crunchy, sort of like a meringue-based cake, all topped with a buttery raspberry frosting. The cake has lots of added egg whites so that the ground almonds won't weigh it down and turn it tough.

For the cake

22 tablespoons (2¾ sticks) cool unsalted butter, cut into small chunks, plus additional for the sheet pan
2¼ cups plus 2 tablespoons cake flour, plus additional for the sheet pan
2 teaspoons baking powder
5 large egg whites, at room temperature
½ teaspoon salt
2 cups plus 2 tablespoons granulated white sugar
1¼ cups finely ground almonds
1 cup whole or 2% milk
1 teaspoon almond extract

1. Position the rack in the center of the oven. Heat the oven to 350°F. Generously butter and lightly flour the inside of a 13 x 18-inch lipped sheet pan.

2. Whisk the cake flour and baking powder in a medium bowl until uniform.

3. Using a handheld electric mixer or a stand mixer with the whisk attachment, beat the egg whites and salt in a second bowl at low speed until foamy, then increase the speed to high and beat until you can make droopy peaks, about 2 minutes. Set aside.

4. Using a handheld electric mixer with clean, dry beaters or a stand mixer with the paddle attachment, beat the butter and sugar in a large bowl at medium speed until smooth, creamy, and even a little fluffy, about 5 minutes. Scrape down the inside of the bowl, then beat in the ground almonds until uniform.

5. Turn off the mixer and pour the flour mixture evenly on top of the batter. Beat at medium speed while slowly pouring in the milk; continue beating until there are no bits of dry flour in the batter. Beat in the almond extract for a few seconds.

6. Scrape down and remove the beaters or paddle. Using a silicone spatula, fold in the beaten egg whites in slow, deliberate arcs, taking care not to deflate them too much but getting them uniform if a bit streaky. Using an offset spatula, spread the batter evenly into the prepared pan.

7. Bake until a toothpick or cake tester inserted into the center of the cake comes out clean, about 24 minutes. Cool in the pan on a wire rack to room temperature, about 1½ hours.

For the buttercream

24 tablespoons (3 sticks) unsalted butter, softened to room temperature
⅔ cup seedless raspberry jam
½ cup heavy cream
2 teaspoons vanilla extract
1 teaspoon raspberry flavoring, optional
½ teaspoon salt
3½ to 5 cups confectioners' sugar

1. Using a handheld electric mixer or a stand mixer with the whisk attachment, beat the butter and jam in a large bowl at medium speed until smooth and creamy, about 2 minutes.

2. Beat in the cream, vanilla, raspberry flavoring, if desired, and salt until smooth. Turn off the mixer, add 3 cups of the confectioners' sugar, and beat at low speed until smooth.

3. Continue beating in more confectioners' sugar in ¼-cup increments until the frosting is spreadable and can hold its shape on the side of a spatula. Using an offset spatula, spread and smooth the frosting over the cooled cake.

TESTER NOTES

Make sure the bowl used for those egg whites is scrupulously dry, not a speck of moisture anywhere, so the whites can rise to their full volume. For the best loft, those egg whites should be at room temperature. Separate them from the yolks and set them in a bowl on the counter for 20 minutes.

PINE NUT CAKE WITH LEMON BUTTERCREAM

Once again, we've used melted butter for a denser texture and crumb—but this time we lightened the cake considerably with beaten egg whites. It's a compromise to give us a texture more in keeping with a traditional sheet cake while still being loaded with pine nuts. Those can be absurdly expensive. Look for them in bulk at Italian markets or from their online suppliers. Or just look in the nut section of your supermarket, rather than buying those little bottles of pine nuts in the spice aisle.

For the cake

16 tablespoons (2 sticks) unsalted butter, melted and cooled to room temperature, plus additional for the sheet pan
2½ cups all-purpose flour
1 teaspoon baking powder
1½ cups pine nuts
4 large eggs plus 4 large egg whites, at room temperature
½ teaspoon salt
1⅓ cups granulated white sugar
1 cup packed light brown sugar
4 teaspoons finely grated lemon zest
1 teaspoon vanilla extract

1. Position the rack in the center of the oven. Heat the oven to 350°F. Generously butter the inside of a 13 x 18-inch lipped sheet pan.

2. Whisk the flour and baking powder in a medium bowl until uniform.

3. Toast the pine nuts in a dry skillet over medium-low heat, stirring occasionally, until lightly browned and fragrant, about 3 minutes. Pour

into a large bowl and cool for 15 minutes while you beat the egg whites and prepare the batter.

4. Using a handheld electric mixer or a stand mixer with the whisk attachment, beat the egg whites and salt in a second large bowl at low speed until foamy. Increase the speed to high and beat until you can make droopy peaks. Continue beating at high speed while adding ⅓ cup of the white sugar in four additions, until you can make stiff, glossy peaks. Set aside.

5. Using a handheld mixer with clean, dry beaters or a stand mixer with the paddle attachment, beat the whole eggs, brown sugar, and the remaining 1 cup white sugar in a large bowl at medium speed until you can make wide ribbons, about 4 minutes.

6. Scrape down and remove the beaters or paddle. Using a silicone spatula, fold in the melted butter, lemon zest, and vanilla until uniform. Pour in the flour mixture and fold just until there are no dry specks. Fold in the pine nuts until uniform.

7. Fold half of the beaten egg whites into the batter until uniform. Then fold in the remaining beaten egg whites in long, slow arcs, just until well distributed but not deflated too much. There may be a few white streaks visible. Using the silicone spatula, spread the batter evenly into the prepared pan.

8. Bake until firm to the touch and a toothpick or cake tester inserted into the center of the cake comes out clean, about 30 minutes. Cool in the pan on a wire rack to room temperature, about 2 hours.

For the buttercream

8 tablespoons (1 stick) unsalted butter, softened to room temperature
8 ounces full-fat cream cheese, softened to room temperature
4 to 5 cups confectioners' sugar
¼ cup fresh lemon juice
1 teaspoon lemon extract
¼ teaspoon salt

1. Using a handheld electric mixer or a stand mixer with the whisk attachment, beat the butter, cream cheese, and 2 cups of the confectioners' sugar in a large bowl at low speed for 1 minute. Increase the speed to medium and beat until smooth, about 1 more minute.

2. Beat in the lemon juice, lemon extract, and salt. Turn off the mixer, add 2 more cups confectioners' sugar, and beat until smooth, adding more confectioners' sugar in 2-tablespoon increments until the frosting is spreadable and can hold its shape on the side of a spatula. Using an offset spatula, spread and smooth the frosting over the cooled cake.

TESTER NOTES
If you like, skip the frosting. Instead, slice pieces of the cooled cake into squares and fry them in melted butter in a skillet over medium heat until lightly browned, about 3 minutes, turning once. Top each piece with a little purchased chocolate sauce or orange marmalade.

ALMOND-CORNMEAL CAKE WITH ORANGE GLAZE

Here's a great trick that gives lots of flavor to this grainy cake: grind the tangerine, rind and all (no seeds, please) right into the sugar. Doing so makes this a ridiculously perfumy cake, a great treat in late winter when citrus is about the only good choice for fresh fruit in the supermarket. The cornmeal adds a rustic texture, sort of like a polenta cake. We felt that a heavy frosting went too far but a sweet and tangy glaze is the perfect topping. Feel free to break out the vin santo!

For the cake

1 cup plus 2 tablespoons canola or vegetable oil, plus additional for the sheet pan
2 cups whole almonds
1½ cups granulated white sugar
1 small tangerine, quartered and seeded
3 large eggs, at room temperature
¾ cup whole milk
½ teaspoon almond extract
¾ cup all-purpose flour
¾ cup yellow cornmeal

1. Position the rack in the center of the oven. Heat the oven to 350°F. Generously oil the inside of a 13 x 18-inch lipped sheet pan.

2. Spread the almonds on a second lipped sheet pan. Toast the nuts in the oven until lightly browned and fragrant, stirring a few times, about 10 minutes. Put the nuts in a food processor and cool for 20 minutes.

3. Cover the food processor and grind the nuts into a coarse flour. Pour the ground almonds into a small bowl. Do not wash the food processor.

4. Put the sugar and tangerine quarters in the food processor. Cover and process until the tangerine has been ground into the sugar. Scrape this mixture into a large bowl or the bowl of a stand mixer.

5. Add the eggs to the tangerine mixture. Using a handheld mixer or a stand mixer with the whisk attachment, beat at medium speed until you can make wide ribbons, about 5 minutes.

6. Beat in the oil in a slow drizzle until smooth, then beat in the milk and almond extract. Scrape down and remove the beaters or whisk.

7. Using a silicone spatula, fold in the ground nuts until well combined, then fold in the flour and cornmeal just until moistened. Using the same spatula, scrape and spread the batter evenly into the prepared pan.

8. Bake until puffed and set, and until a toothpick or cake tester inserted into the center of the cake comes out clean, about 25 minutes. Cool in the pan on a wire rack to room temperature, about 2 hours.

For the glaze

1½ to 2 cups confectioners' sugar
6 tablespoons (¾ stick) unsalted butter, melted and cooled to room temperature
4½ teaspoons frozen orange juice concentrate, thawed
1 tablespoon light corn syrup
2 teaspoons finely grated orange zest
½ teaspoon vanilla extract
½ teaspoon orange extract, optional

1. Whisk 1½ cups of the confectioners' sugar, the melted butter, orange juice concentrate, corn syrup, orange zest, vanilla, and orange extract, if using, in a medium bowl until it can hold its shape on the tines of the whisk, adding more confectioners' sugar in 1-tablespoon increments as necessary. Drizzle over the top of the cooled cake.

TESTER NOTES

For a more professional look, put the glaze in a zipper-lock plastic bag; seal it closed. Snip off the corner, then squeeze (or pipe) the glaze over the cake.

SPICED WALNUT CAKE

Like the previous cake, this one has no frosting. Instead, you'll make a yogurt-based spice and nut cake, then poke holes in it before brushing a hot sugar syrup across the top. The glaze seeps down into the crumb and makes this the most coffee cake–like cake in this chapter.

½ cup plus 2 tablespoons canola or vegetable oil plus additional for the sheet pan
3½ cups walnut pieces (about 1 pound)
4 cups all-purpose flour
4½ teaspoons baking powder
1½ teaspoons ground cinnamon
1 teaspoon ground cloves
1 teaspoon baking soda
½ teaspoon freshly grated nutmeg
½ teaspoon salt
4 large eggs, at room temperature
1½ cups packed light brown sugar
1⅓ cups plain full-fat Greek yogurt
1 tablespoon finely grated orange zest plus 2 cups fresh orange juice
¾ cup packed dark brown sugar
3 tablespoons unsalted butter

1. Position the rack in the center of the oven. Heat the oven to 350°F. Generously oil the inside of a 13 x 18-inch lipped sheet pan.

2. Sprinkle the walnut pieces on a second lipped sheet pan. Toast the nuts in the oven, stirring occasionally, until lightly browned and fragrant, about 10 minutes. Cool to room temperature, about 30 minutes.

3. Whisk the flour, baking powder, cinnamon, cloves, baking soda, nutmeg, and salt in a medium bowl until uniform.

4. Roughly chop 1½ cups of the toasted walnuts and set aside. Finely chop the remaining toasted walnuts.

5. Using a handheld electric mixer or a stand mixer with the paddle attachment, beat the eggs and light brown sugar in a large bowl at medium speed until you can make wide ribbons, about 5 minutes.

6. Scrape down the inside of the bowl, then beat in the yogurt until smooth. Beat in the oil, orange zest, and 1 cup of the orange juice until uniform.

7. Beat in the finely chopped walnuts. Turn off the mixer, add the flour mixture, and beat at low speed just until there are no bits of dry flour. Using an offset spatula, spread the batter evenly into the prepared pan.

8. Bake until lightly browned and set to the touch, and until a toothpick or cake tester inserted into the center of the cake comes out clean, 20 to 24 minutes.

9. As the cake bakes, bring the remaining 1 cup orange juice, the dark brown sugar, and the butter to a boil in a small saucepan set over medium heat, stirring often until the sugar dissolves, then less frequently thereafter. Continue to boil undisturbed until reduced to a thick syrup, about 6 minutes.

10. Transfer the hot cake in its pan to a wire rack. Use a metal or bamboo skewer to poke tiny holes all across the top of the cake. Brush the buttery syrup over the top of the cake while both are still hot. Sprinkle the top with the roughly chopped walnuts while the syrup is warm and sticky.

TESTER NOTES

Make lots of holes across the cake. Space them evenly apart, about 1 inch or so.

HAZELNUT CAKE WITH VANILLA FRENCH BUTTERCREAM

Now things get serious! Not the cake—although it's pretty fine: light and tender, with a sturdy crumb. Notice that the butter for it should be at room temperature. We actually want very little air beaten into it for a more substantial texture. (No, instead we mean the buttercream gets serious!) This is the real deal, no mere mix of confectioners' sugar and butter. This is how a French pastry chef would make it. The results are incredibly creamy and smooth. But watch the technique, especially the various stated temperatures. If you follow our advice exactly, you'll end up with the richest, most creamy frosting in this book.

For the cake

20 tablespoons (2½ sticks) unsalted butter, softened to room temperature, plus additional for the sheet pan
2½ cups cake flour
2½ teaspoons baking powder
1 teaspoon salt
1½ cups toasted, skinned hazelnuts
2½ cups granulated white sugar
7 large eggs plus 1 large egg white, at room temperature
½ cup whole milk
2 teaspoons vanilla extract

1. Position the rack in the center of the oven. Heat the oven to 350°F. Generously butter the inside of a 13 x 18-inch lipped sheet pan.

2. Whisk the flour, baking powder, and salt in a medium bowl until uniform.

3. Process the hazelnuts in a food processor until the consistency of coarse cornmeal.

4. Using a handheld electric mixer or a stand mixer with the paddle attachment, beat the butter and sugar in a large bowl at medium speed until creamy and light, about 3 minutes. Beat in the eggs one at a time, followed by the egg white.

5. Beat in the milk and vanilla until smooth, then beat in the ground nuts. Scrape down and remove the beaters or paddle. Using a silicone spatula, fold in the flour mixture just until there are no bits of dry flour. Using an offset spatula, spread the batter evenly into the prepared pan.

6. Bake until set to the touch, and until a toothpick or cake tester inserted into the center of the cake comes out clean, 18 to 22 minutes. Cool in the pan on a wire rack to room temperature, about 1½ hours.

For the buttercream

6 large egg yolks, at room temperature
¾ cup granulated white sugar
½ cup light corn syrup
32 tablespoons (4 sticks) unsalted butter, softened to room temperature
2 teaspoons vanilla extract
3 tablespoons vanilla-flavored liqueur, such as Tuaca or Licor 43, optional

1. Using a handheld electric mixer with clean, dry beaters or a stand mixer with the whisk attachment, beat the egg yolks in a large bowl at medium speed until light and pale yellow, about 2 minutes.

2. Melt the sugar into the corn syrup in a large skillet set over medium-high heat, stirring until the sugar dissolves; then cook undisturbed until the mixture comes to a boil. Boil for 1 minute.

3. With the mixer at medium speed, slowly and steadily drizzle the hot sugar syrup into the egg yolks. Continue beating at medium speed until the mixture is room temperature, for at least 10 minutes, maybe longer.

4. Beat in the butter 1 tablespoon at a time, working slowly and efficiently. Beat in the vanilla and liqueur, if using, until smooth. Smooth and spread the buttercream over the cooled cake.

TESTER NOTES

There are two tricks to the buttercream. One, beat in that sugar syrup while it's very hot—and in the slowest drizzle. Watch out: the mixture is scalding hot. Two, continue beating the mixture until it's room temperature before you add the butter. Cup your hands around the outside of the bowl. Turn off the mixer and stick your clean and dry finger into the mixture in several places. There must be no residual heat or the butter will melt and the buttercream will break. If so, there's no fixing it.

COFFEE
CAKES &
CHEESECAKES

Now we've stretched the concept of a sheet cake almost to its breaking point. (Don't worry: we'll go all the way in the last chapter of this book.) Any of these is sure to please a crowd of friends and relatives when you have them over for a deck party or a game of cards. But take care: the cheesecakes are actually sturdier than the coffee cakes. Plan on serving the latter the day you make them, maybe the next morning at the latest.

The Lay of the Land

As a general rule, a coffee cake is an unfrosted single-layer cake with a denser crumb than a standard cake. It's got a slightly more rustic, even sandy texture. The batter tends to be drier and a bit less coherent.

In other words, it'll give your mixer a good workout. Don't strain the motor. If you find it pulling or bucking, you may have to work in batches, especially at the end when you add the flour mixture to the beaten butter mixture. To do so, remove half of the butter mixture, then add half the flour mixture to it and beat it together. Scrape this mixture into a second bowl, then blend the second half of each before finally stirring the two together with a wooden spoon and lots of shoulder work.

A coffee cake is also by and large sweeter than a standard sheet cake. Perhaps that's why it's rarely frosted. Rather, it's usually got some sort of crunchy topping, some butter/ sugar/nut combination that gives it a toothy bite. The crunch and crumble toppings here are not mix-and-match affairs, as were most of the frostings for the sheet cakes. These toppings were designed to match the density of the batter at hand. Some can sink in an alternate, lighter batter and would then ruin that coffee cake as it baked.

On the other hand, a sheet cheesecake is relatively easy to prepare and surprisingly not temperamental in the oven. Although it's much thinner than a standard cheesecake, don't throw it shade. It's a superrich cream cheese layer over a sturdy crust (often a graham cracker one but sometimes made from Oreo cookies or even animal crackers). Because the cheesecake itself is relatively thin, you're free to add toppings galore. It may well be rank excess to put whipped cream on a standard, tall slice of cheesecake. Not so with a piece of a sheet cheesecake. Dollop away!

The Best Crunch or Crumble Topping

There are plenty here and the secret to their success lies in the technique. Take a little of the crunch or crumble mixture (a crumble is slightly thicker, slightly more like dough) and squeeze it into a lump in your palm, then break that lump into lots of little pebbles and sandy bits that you scatter across the top of the batter.

Doing so is a lot of work, the most time-consuming part of these recipes, but yields the most even and satisfying topping for a coffee cake.

Cold and Room-Temperature Ingredients

For the best results, pay attention to the difference between what's to be cold and what's to be room temperature in these recipes. As in almost all the sheet cake recipes, we use cold butter to get more air beaten into a coffee cake batter.

However, we almost always call for room-temperature cream cheese in cheesecakes for the opposite reason: we don't want too much air in the mix so the cake becomes denser, a little chewy. Plus, cold ingredients can shock the eggs in certain types of batters, resulting in gummier or tougher end results.

The Cheesecake Warning

Cheesecakes have to chill in the refrigerator so they can set properly. You must then make them several hours, or up to a day, in advance. Read the recipe to determine the requirements.

Make room in your fridge. Since a sheet cheesecake will need to chill before you can serve it, you'll probably have to clean out a shelf. If you've got a side-by-side, you're going to wish you didn't. Stick an empty sheet pan in there first to make sure you've got clearance. Better safe than sorry.

You can, of course, set a cheesecake outdoors on a chilly day: around 40°F but certainly not near or below freezing. We can't. We live in the woods and would be inviting furry well-wishers to a party. But you may find yourself in a more urban setting. Beware the neighbors, too.

And Finally . . .

These specialties may not be where you start out in this book but we'll bet you'll come back to these more often than you can imagine. Once we were done writing this book, we made the Classic Cheesecake and a couple of the sheet coffee cakes more times than any other recipe.

CRANBERRY-ORANGE COFFEE CAKE WITH GINGER CRUNCH

Let's start with a rather straightforward coffee cake, great on a chilly day. It's topped with a crunch, not a bumpier crumble. In other words, this topping is a little sandy. It'll melt into the cake a bit as it bakes, then firm back up to a crunchy top when cool. The amount of ground ginger is variable, depending on how "spicy" you want the topping.

For the crunch

1 cup plus 1 tablespoon light brown sugar
5 tablespoons plus 1½ teaspoons all-purpose flour
1 to 2 teaspoons ground dried ginger
¼ teaspoon freshly grated nutmeg
¼ teaspoon salt
4 tablespoons (½ stick) cold unsalted butter, cut into small chunks

1. Mix the brown sugar, flour, ginger, nutmeg, and salt in a medium bowl. Use a pastry cutter or a fork to cut the bits of butter into this mixture, repeatedly pushing them through the tines and into the brown sugar mixture, wiping the tines clean, and going at it again, until the whole thing resembles coarse cornmeal with no individual bits of butter visible.

For the coffee cake

12 tablespoons (1½ sticks) cold unsalted butter, cut into small chunks, plus additional for the sheet pan
3 cups all-purpose flour, plus additional for the sheet pan
2 teaspoons baking powder
½ teaspoon salt
1⅓ cups granulated white sugar
1 tablespoon finely grated orange zest plus ¼ cup fresh orange juice
4 large eggs, at room temperature
1⅓ cups full-fat sour cream
1 teaspoon vanilla extract
1 teaspoon orange extract
9 ounces frozen cranberries (about 2 cups)

1. Position the rack in the center of the oven. Heat the oven to 350°F. Generously butter and lightly flour the inside of a 13 x 18-inch lipped sheet pan.

2. Whisk the flour, baking powder, and salt in a medium bowl until uniform.

3. Using a handheld electric mixer or a stand mixer with the paddle attachment, beat the butter, sugar, and orange zest in a large bowl at medium speed until creamy and velvety, about 4 minutes.

4. Scrape down the inside of the bowl, then beat in the eggs one at a time. Beat in the sour cream, vanilla, and orange extract until uniform and smooth.

5. Turn off the mixer and pour the flour mixture evenly on top of the batter. Beat at medium speed while slowly pouring in the orange juice; continue beating just until there are no bits of dry flour in the batter.

6. Scrape down and remove the beaters or paddle. Fold in the cranberries with a silicone spatula until evenly distributed in the thick batter. Put your shoulder into it; the batter will be very stiff.

7. Using an offset spatula, spread the thick batter evenly into the prepared pan. Clean and dry your hands, then squeeze small handfuls of the crumble topping into clumps before breaking each up as you sand them evenly over the batter.

8. Bake until firm and set to the touch, and until a toothpick or cake tester inserted into the cake comes out clean, 30 to 33 minutes. Cool in the pan on a wire rack for at least 20 minutes before slicing into squares to serve warm.

TESTER NOTES
Using frozen cranberries ensures that they stay whole. However, they also make the batter ridiculously thick. You'll need to use good force to get them folded in and to get the batter spread into the prepared pan.

SOUR CREAM COFFEE CAKE WITH CINNAMON CRUMBLE

This one's probably the most classic coffee cake of the bunch, our version of Drake's coffee cake. If you live around New York City, you'll know what we're talking about. If you've watched Seinfeld, you'll know, too. And if you don't, or haven't, then this one's a fairly tender, light cake with a crunchy, buttery, cinnamon-scented topping. In fact, there's so much topping that the cake collapses a bit under its weight, getting softer and a little chewier right underneath.

For the crumble
3 cups all-purpose flour
1⅓ cups packed light brown sugar
2 tablespoons ground cinnamon
½ teaspoon salt
16 tablespoons (2 sticks) unsalted butter, melted and cooled to room temperature
1 tablespoon vanilla extract

1. Mix the flour, brown sugar, cinnamon, and salt in a large bowl until uniform. Stir in the melted butter and vanilla until the mixture is a crumbly amalgam.

For the coffee cake
19 tablespoons (2 sticks plus 3 tablespoons) cool unsalted butter, cut into small chunks, plus additional for the sheet pan
4¾ cups all-purpose flour
1¼ teaspoons baking powder
1 teaspoon salt
½ teaspoon baking soda
1⅔ cups granulated white sugar
⅔ cup packed light brown sugar
3 large eggs plus 1 large egg yolk, at room temperature

4½ teaspoons vanilla extract
1¾ cups plus 1 tablespoon full-fat sour cream

1. Position the rack in the center of the oven. Heat the oven to 325°F. Generously butter the inside of a 13 x 18-inch lipped sheet pan.

2. Whisk the flour, baking powder, salt, and baking soda in a medium bowl until uniform.

3. Using a handheld electric mixer or a stand mixer with the paddle attachment, beat the butter and both sugars in a large bowl at medium speed until creamy and light, about 5 minutes.

4. Beat in the eggs one at a time, then beat in the egg yolk and vanilla until uniform. Scrape down the inside of the bowl and beat in the sour cream until smooth.

5. Add the flour mixture and beat at low speed until the batter is quite thick, about like a wet paste. Use an offset spatula to spread the thick batter evenly into the prepared pan. Clean and dry your hands, then squeeze small handfuls of the crumble topping into oblong clumps before breaking each up as you scatter the small bits over the batter. Continue until the top is evenly covered in a little "sand" and lots of small "pebbles."

6. Bake until set and browned, and until a toothpick or cake tester inserted into the center of the cake comes out clean, 35 to 38 minutes. Cool in the pan on a wire rack for at least 20 minutes before slicing into squares to serve warm.

TESTER NOTES

Make the crumbles on top about the size of shelled peanuts with finer bits around them—lots and lots of little tidbits scattered everywhere.

BANANA–CHOCOLATE CHIP COFFEE CAKE WITH COCONUT CRUMBLE

Because bananas add so much moisture, this batter comes close to being a sheet cake once it's baked (rather than a more standard coffee cake with a slightly sandy crumb). It's not quite like banana bread, more like the old-fashioned banana cakes our grandmothers once made. But never fear: the coconut topping turns it back into a coffee cake. The crumble is made with coconut oil, which is often solid at room temperature, quite a bit harder than solid vegetable shortening. You'll need to scrape it out of the jar with a fork and pack it into the measuring cup.

For the crumble
1¼ cups all-purpose flour
⅔ cup coconut oil
⅔ cup packed dark brown sugar
1 teaspoon ground cinnamon
At least 2 tablespoons heavy cream

1. Put the flour, coconut oil, brown sugar, and cinnamon in a large food processor. Cover and pulse until well combined, about like coarse cornmeal.

2. Add 2 tablespoons cream, cover, and pulse until the mixture becomes a crumbly amalgam that can be squeezed into pieces, adding more cream in ½-tablespoon increments to get the right texture. Do not add too much cream. Test a bit by squeezing it into a little lump between your clean fingers. Once you've got it right, scrape down and remove the blade.

For the coffee cake

¾ cup canola or vegetable oil, plus additional for the sheet pan

3½ cups all-purpose flour

4½ teaspoons baking powder

1 teaspoon salt

1¾ cups plus 2 tablespoons granulated white sugar

4 large eggs, at room temperature

¾ cup plain low-fat or fat-free plain Greek yogurt

1 cup whole or 2% milk

1 tablespoon vanilla extract

2 cups mini chocolate chips

1 tablespoon ground cinnamon

3 ripe medium bananas, peeled and thinly sliced

1. Position the rack in the center of the oven. Heat the oven to 350°F. Generously oil the inside of a 13 x 18-inch lipped sheet pan.

2. Whisk the flour, baking powder, and salt in a medium bowl until uniform. Set aside.

3. Using a handheld electric mixer or a stand mixer with the whisk attachment, beat 1½ cups of the sugar and the eggs in a large bowl at medium speed until you can make wide ribbons, about 6 minutes.

4. Beat in the oil until smooth, then scrape down the inside of the bowl and beat in the yogurt. Turn off the mixer and pour the flour mixture on top. Beat at low speed while slowly pouring in the milk. Add the vanilla and continue beating just until there are no bits of dry flour in the batter. Scrape down and remove the beaters or whisk.

5. Toss the chocolate chips with the remaining 6 tablespoons white sugar and the cinnamon in a small bowl. Using a silicone spatula, gently fold this mixture along with the bananas into the batter just until evenly distributed. There should be streaks of cinnamon sugar.

6. Using an offset spatula, spread the batter evenly into the prepared pan. Clean your hands, then squeeze bits of the crumble mixture into oblongs in your palm before breaking them up and sprinkling them evenly across the top, making little pebbles, slightly larger chunks, and coarse sandy bits all over.

7. Bake until lightly browned and a toothpick or cake tester inserted into the center of the cake without touching a banana slice comes out clean, about 40 minutes. Cool in the pan on a wire rack for at least 20 minutes before slicing into squares to serve.

TESTER NOTES

You'll need to scrape the coconut oil out of the jar with a fork. Pack it into the measuring cup to get the right amount.

GLUTEN-FREE BANANA COFFEE CAKE
WITH COCONUT MERINGUE

This soft, moist coffee cake gets a surprise topping: a thin Italian meringue, a cooked confection with a pillowy marshmallow texture (rather than the more standard meringue that's baked on top of an all-American pie). In fact, you could pick up this Italian meringue technique and put the topping on almost all but the most delicate sheet cakes or coffee cakes in this book.

For the coffee cake
¾ cup almond oil, plus additional for the sheet pan
1½ cups buckwheat flour
1 cup oat flour
1 cup white rice flour
1 cup almond flour or very finely ground almonds
½ cup cornstarch
1 tablespoon baking powder
1 teaspoon salt
1½ cups packed light brown sugar
1 cup granulated white sugar
6 large eggs, at room temperature
5 ripe medium bananas, peeled and cut into 1-inch pieces
1 teaspoon vanilla extract
½ teaspoon almond extract
2 cups finely ground unsweetened shredded coconut

1. Position the rack in the center of the oven. Heat the oven to 350°F. Generously oil the inside of a 13 x 18-inch lipped sheet pan.

2. Whisk the buckwheat flour, oat flour, rice flour, almond flour, cornstarch, baking powder, and salt in a medium bowl.

3. Using a handheld electric mixer or a stand mixer with the paddle attachment, beat the oil and both sugars in a large bowl at medium speed until creamy, about 3 minutes.

4. Scrape down the inside of the bowl, then beat in the eggs one at a time. Beat in the bananas, vanilla, and almond extracts until uniform. The batter may look broken at this stage.

5. Turn off the mixer and add the buckwheat flour mixture. Beat at medium-low speed until smooth, then beat in the shredded coconut. Using an offset spatula, spread the thick batter evenly into the prepared pan.

6. Bake until puffed and set, and until a toothpick inserted into the center of the cake comes out clean, 28 to 30 minutes. Cool in the pan on a wire rack to room temperature, about 1½ hours.

For the meringue
1¼ cups granulated white sugar
¼ cup water
5 large egg whites, at room temperature
½ teaspoon salt
1½ cups finely ground unsweetened shredded coconut
½ teaspoon almond extract

1. Clip a candy thermometer to the inside of a small saucepan. Add the sugar and water; bring to a boil over medium-high heat, stirring often at first, then leaving undisturbed once the sugar has dissolved. Continue boiling until the temperature reaches 250°F, about 4 minutes.

2. Meanwhile, using a handheld electric mixer or a stand mixer with the whisk attachment, beat the egg whites and salt in a large bowl at low speed until foamy, then increase the speed to high and continue beating until you can make soft peaks.

3. Reduce the speed to medium and beat in the hot sugar syrup in dribs and drabs at first, then in a thin, steady stream. Too much at once will deflate the egg whites.

4. Once all the syrup has been added, continue beating until the mixture is warm to the touch through the bowl (about 100°F), about 5 minutes. Beat in the coconut and almond extract. Spread the meringue over the top of the cake.

5. Position the rack 4 to 6 inches from the broiler; heat the broiler. Broil until the meringue is lightly browned, less than 1 minute. Cool a few minutes before serving.

TESTER NOTES
Although it doesn't look like there's a gap between steps 2 and 3, there may well be. If the sugar syrup is not at the right temperature, stop beating the egg white mixture until the syrup is ready. You do not want to dry out the egg whites or even turn them into stiff peaks.

GLUTEN-FREE COFFEE CAKE WITH ALMOND-BUTTER CRUNCH

There's no reason to feel deprived if you're doing without gluten—or if you know someone who is. In fact, there's no reason to be gluten-intolerant to make this rich coffee cake with a sturdy, toothy texture and intense, surprisingly "grainy" flavor. It's also got both a buttery almond topping and a tart lemon glaze over that for the joy of sheer excess. Even if you don't have dietary concerns, just make it and don't tell anyone it's gluten-free.

For the crunch
1½ cups chopped whole almonds
½ cup almond butter
1 cup packed light brown sugar
3 tablespoons unsalted butter, melted and cooled to room temperature
1 tablespoon heavy cream
2 teaspoons ground cinnamon

1. Mix the almonds, almond butter, brown sugar, melted butter, cream, and cinnamon in a medium bowl until uniform. Set aside.

For the coffee cake
21 tablespoons (2 sticks plus 5 tablespoons) cool unsalted butter, cut into chunks, plus additional for the sheet pan
1¾ cups buckwheat flour
1 cup white rice flour
¾ cup oat flour
½ cup cornstarch
1 tablespoon baking powder
½ teaspoon salt

2 cups granulated white sugar

4 large eggs, at room temperature

2 cups full-fat sour cream

2 teaspoons vanilla extract

1. Position the rack in the center of the oven. Heat the oven to 350°F. Generously butter the inside of a 13 x 18-inch lipped sheet pan.

2. Whisk the buckwheat flour, rice flour, oat flour, cornstarch, baking powder, and salt in a second medium bowl until uniform.

3. Using a handheld electric mixer or a stand mixer with the paddle attachment, beat the butter and sugar in a large bowl at medium speed until very creamy, even fluffy, about 6 minutes.

4. Scrape down the inside of the bowl, then beat in the eggs one at a time. Beat in the sour cream and vanilla until smooth.

5. Turn off the mixer, add the buckwheat flour mixture, and beat at low speed until well combined. Using an offset spatula, spread the thick batter evenly into the prepared pan. Clean and dry your hands. Squeeze the almond mixture into cohesive, oblong lumps and crumble these over the top of the batter as little stones and pebbles.

6. Bake until puffed and set, and until a toothpick inserted into the center of the cake comes out clean, about 30 minutes. Cool in the pan on a wire rack to room temperature, about 1½ hours.

For the glaze

2 tablespoons unsalted butter, melted and cooled to room temperature

2 tablespoons fresh lemon juice

Up to 2 cups confectioner's sugar

Stir the butter and lemon juice in a small bowl, then add 1 cup of the confectioners' sugar and stir well, adding more confectioners' sugar in 2-tablespoon increments, to form a loose, wet glaze. Drizzle the glaze from the tines of a flatware fork all over the cooled cake, making thicker and thinner ribbons across the top.

TESTER NOTES

Make sure the nonwheat flours and the baking powder are certified gluten-free, if this is a concern to you and yours. Buckwheat flour can go rancid quickly. Store it in a tightly sealed container in the freezer for up to four months.

CINNAMON ROLL CAKE

Imagine if you thinned out the dough for super-buttery cinnamon rolls and baked the whole thing in a sheet pan. Okay, we can't either. But this sheet coffee cake tastes like a giant cinnamon roll, right down to the firm outer coating and the simple glaze on top. But there's no yeast.

24 tablespoons (3 sticks) cool unsalted butter, cut into small chunks, plus additional for the sheet pan
3¾ cups plus 3 tablespoons all-purpose flour
1¼ cups granulated white sugar
2 tablespoons baking powder
½ teaspoon salt
2½ cups whole milk
1½ cups solid vegetable shortening, melted and cooled to room temperature
2 large eggs plus 1 large egg white, at room temperature
3½ teaspoons vanilla extract
1½ cups packed dark brown sugar
2 tablespoons ground cinnamon
3 to 4 cups confectioners' sugar

1. Position the rack in the center of the oven. Heat the oven to 350°F. Generously butter the inside of a 13 x 18-inch lipped sheet pan.

2. Whisk 3¾ cups of the flour, the white sugar, baking powder, and salt in a large bowl until uniform. Whisk in 2 cups of the milk, the melted and cooled shortening, eggs, egg white, and 2½ teaspoons of the vanilla until evenly and thoroughly combined.

3. Using a handheld electric mixer or a stand mixer with the paddle attachment, beat the butter, brown sugar, cinnamon, and the remaining 3 tablespoons flour in a medium bowl at medium speed until creamy and light, about 2 minutes.

4. Take out about a third of this butter mixture and set aside. Make olive-sized balls out of the remaining butter mixture. Drop them into the flour batter from step 2 and gently fold them in with a silicone spatula. There should be streaks in the batter and even some buttery chunks.

5. Using an offset spatula, spread this batter into the prepared sheet pan. Dot the reserved butter mixture over the top of the batter by breaking it up into small dribs and drabs. Use a paring knife to swirl these around and through the batter without scratching the pan just below.

6. Bake until set to the touch, and until a toothpick or cake tester inserted into the center of the cake comes out clean, about 30 minutes. Cool in the pan on a wire rack to room temperature, about 2 hours.

7. Before serving, whisk 3 cups of the confectioners' sugar, the remaining ½ cup milk, and the remaining 1 teaspoon vanilla extract in a large bowl until thick enough to drizzle on top of the cake. Whisk in more confectioners' sugar in 2-tablespoon increments for the right consistency, a loose, wet mixture that will fall off the tines of a fork and puddle into little pools that don't immediately run.

8. Drizzle this glaze off the whisk and all over the cooled cake, making squiggles across the top rather than one solid mass of glaze.

TESTER NOTES
You must cool the cake thoroughly in step 6 or the glaze will break and run across its surface.

CLASSIC CHEESECAKE

Yes, a sheet cheesecake is thinner than a traditional cheesecake. But that just means you've got a better crust-to-cream ratio (if you like crusts the way we do). We added a little flour to the batter because we needed to stabilize the set across such a wide expanse. Listen, no one will notice because the results are ridiculously velvety. And here's a bonus: sheet cheesecakes rarely crack because they're not felled by their own weight in the pan.

Graham Cracker Crust (page 117)
2½ pounds full-fat cream cheese, softened to
    room temperature
1 cup packed light brown sugar
1 cup granulated white sugar
5 large eggs, at room temperature
1 cup full-fat sour cream
1 tablespoon fresh lemon juice
1 tablespoon vanilla extract
¼ cup all-purpose flour
2¼ pounds fresh strawberries, hulled and thinly
    sliced (about 6 cups)
Sweetened Whipped Cream (page 59)

1. Position the rack in the center of the oven. Heat the oven to 350°F. Prepare and shape the crust as directed in a buttered 13 x 18-inch lipped sheet pan.

2. Using a handheld electric mixer or a stand mixer with the paddle attachment, beat the cream cheese, brown sugar, and ¾ cup of the white sugar in a large bowl at medium speed until light and fluffy, about 5 minutes.

3. Beat in the eggs one at a time; then beat in the sour cream, lemon juice, and vanilla until smooth. Finally, beat in the flour until dissolved. Pour and scrape this mixture evenly into the crust.

4. Bake until slightly puffed and set if still a little jiggly at the center, 30 to 35 minutes. Cool in the pan on a wire rack to room temperature, about 1 hour. Cover lightly with plastic wrap and refrigerate for at least 3 hours or overnight, until firm and chilled.

5. Mix the sliced strawberries and the remaining ¼ cup white sugar in a medium bowl until the sugar begins to dissolve. Macerate at room temperature, stirring two or three times, for 30 minutes.

6. Slice the cheesecake into squares and serve each with a dollop of the whipped cream and some of the macerated strawberries, as well as their juice.

TESTER NOTES
Watch that set: the cheesecake should not be liquid at its center but instead just able to wobble a bit when the side of the pan is tapped.

CHOCOLATE CHIP–RICOTTA CHEESECAKE

Grated orange zest sets off the chocolate and gives this cheesecake a bit of unexpected lightness, despite all the eggs and the whole-milk ricotta. (Plus, chocolate and orange are such a classic combo!) The ricotta gives this cheesecake a more rustic texture: not quite as smooth nor as sour as a traditional cheesecake, certainly sweeter with a slight graininess to the set. The results are a bit softer than a standard cheesecake, a little bit mousse-like and perhaps more appealing after a big dinner. One warning: the concoction must "ripen" in the fridge for at least twelve hours before serving, not only to improve the set, but also to blend the flavors.

Single-crust version of All-Butter Crust
    (page 147)
8 large eggs, at room temperature
2 cups granulated white sugar
2 pounds whole-milk ricotta, at room
    temperature
2 tablespoons finely grated orange zest
1 tablespoon vanilla extract
½ teaspoon salt
¼ cup all-purpose flour
15 ounces semisweet or milk chocolate chips
    (about 2½ cups)

1. Position the rack in the center of the oven. Heat the oven to 350°F. Prepare and shape the crust as directed in a 13 x 18-inch lipped sheet pan.

2. Prick the crust repeatedly with a flatware fork across the flat surface and up the sides. Cover the crust loosely with aluminum foil and bake for 10 minutes. Transfer to a wire rack and immediately remove the foil. Maintain the oven temperature.

3. Using a handheld electric mixer or a stand mixer with the whisk attachment, beat the eggs and sugar in a large bowl at medium speed until you can make wide ribbons that fall off the beaters, about 6 minutes. The mixture should almost double in volume. Beat in the ricotta until smooth.

4. Beat in the orange zest, vanilla, and salt, then beat in the flour until smooth. Scrape down and remove the beaters or whisk. Fold in the chocolate chips with a silicone spatula. Pour and spread the batter into the blind-baked crust.

5. Bake until lightly browned, puffed, and fully set, 25 to 30 minutes. Cool in the pan on a wire rack to room temperature, about 1½ hours. Cover loosely with plastic wrap and refrigerate for at least 12 hours or up to 2 days before serving.

NO-BAKE CHERRY-CHOCOLATE CHEESECAKE

"No-bake" means there's gelatin in the mix to get the cheesecake to set in the fridge. You'll get a creamy filling, a little richer than the standard cheesecake, mostly because of the proteins in that gelatin. (Make sure you use unflavored gelatin, found in the baking aisle, not Jell-O powder.) The ganache, unfortunately, does require a little cooking. Well, you just have to heat the half-and-half before you pour it over chocolate. That's not much! And after that, you chill down the rich ganache before spreading it over the cake.

For the cheesecake

Vanilla Cookie Crust (page 117)
¼ cup sweet or sour cherry juice (not concentrate)
One ¼-ounce package unflavored gelatin
1½ pounds full-fat cream cheese
2 cups cherry jam
½ cup granulated white sugar
½ cup full-fat sour cream
1 tablespoon fresh lemon juice
1 teaspoon vanilla extract
1 teaspoon cherry flavoring or extract, optional

1. Prepare and shape the crust as directed in a buttered 13 x 18-inch lipped sheet pan.

2. Mix the cherry juice and gelatin in a small bowl and set aside until the liquid has been mostly absorbed, about 5 minutes.

3. Put the cream cheese, jam, sugar, sour cream, lemon juice, vanilla, and cherry flavoring, if using, in a large food processor. Cover and process until smooth. Scrape down the inside of the canister, add the gelatin mixture, and process until smooth. (For smaller food processors, work in two batches, halving the gelatin mixture to add it to both. Fold the two batches together in a large bowl until smooth.) Scrape and pour this mixture into the prepared crust. Cover with plastic wrap and refrigerate for at least 8 hours or up to 2 days.

For the ganache

1 cup half-and-half
1½ pounds chopped bittersweet chocolate or bittersweet chocolate chips
1 cup confectioners' sugar

1. At least an hour and a half (or up to one day) before serving, warm the half-and-half in a small saucepan set over medium heat until small bubbles fizz around the inside perimeter.

2. Put the chocolate in a medium bowl, pour in the warmed cream, and stir until melted and smooth. Cool for 20 minutes.

3. Whisk in the confectioners' sugar. Refrigerate until the mixture is spreadable but not stiff, about 20 minutes. Spread evenly over the chilled cheesecake. Chill the topped cheesecake for another 15 minutes before serving.

TESTER NOTES
Don't use bottled lemon juice. It may have been pasteurized and won't be as acidic as the fresh stuff, so the cheesecake will not set.

RASPBERRY-GLAZED CHEESECAKE WITH AN OREO CRUST

Here, we don't doctor the flavor of the ricotta cheesecake with chocolate chips or bits of orange. Rather, we let its slightly sweet, grainy texture stand on its own against a thicker chocolate crust and a sweet, jam-like topping. It's sort of like dipping an Oreo into sweetened ricotta and topping it with jam. No, that doesn't make any sense. Anyway, the results are rich and even beautiful, a sophisticated dessert for any dinner party.

One 19.1-ounce (that is, family size) package Oreo or other chocolate cream sandwich cookies
10 tablespoons (1¼ sticks) unsalted butter, melted and cooled
1¾ pounds full-fat cream cheese, softened to room temperature
1¾ cups plus 2 tablespoons granulated white sugar
1 cup whole-milk ricotta, at room temperature
6 large eggs, at room temperature
4½ teaspoons vanilla extract
5 tablespoons cake flour
1¼ cups seedless raspberry jam

1. Position the rack in the center of the oven. Heat the oven to 325°F.

2. Process the Oreos in batches in a food processor until about the consistency of very coarse sand. Pour the crumbs into a large bowl and stir in the melted butter until moistened.

3. Spread this mixture into a 13 x 18-inch lipped sheet pan. With clean, dry fingers, press the mixture into an even crust across the bottom and up the sides of the pan. Set aside.

4. Using a handheld electric mixer or a stand mixer with the paddle attachment, beat the cream cheese, sugar, and ricotta in a large bowl at medium speed until creamy, light, and even fluffy, about 4 minutes.

5. Beat in the eggs one at a time, then beat in the vanilla until smooth. Beat in the flour at low speed until dissolved. Pour and spread the batter into the prepared crust.

6. Bake until puffed, set, and lightly browned, about 35 minutes. Cool in the pan on a wire rack to room temperature, about 3 hours. Cover tightly and store in the refrigerator for 24 hours before serving.

7. Place the raspberry jam in a microwave-safe medium bowl and microwave on high for about 10 seconds, or until you can stir it with a fork. The jam should not be warm. If it is, cool to room temperature after stirring smooth. Using an offset spatula, spread this glaze evenly over the cooled cheesecake.

TESTER NOTES

If you can't find seedless raspberry jam, use 1½ cups regular raspberry jam. Push it in a fine-mesh sieve set over a bowl, using a silicone spatula to wipe it against the mesh.

CHOCOLATE–CHOCOLATE CHIP CHEESECAKE

This one's got about as much chocolate as we can force into a cheesecake: ground in the crust, melted into the batter, and even shaved on top. We wouldn't want to shortchange any chocolate lovers! Note that the recipe calls for low-fat or fat-free Greek yogurt. Full-fat proved far too rich, almost unctuous.

12 tablespoons (1½ sticks) unsalted butter, melted and cooled, plus additional for the sheet pan

One 14.4-ounce box chocolate graham crackers, ground into crumbs in a food processor (about 4 cups)

¼ cup confectioners' sugar

2 tablespoons whole or 2% milk

1½ pounds full-fat cream cheese, softened to room temperature

1¼ cups granulated white sugar

1 cup plain low-fat or fat-free Greek yogurt

5 large eggs, at room temperature

12 ounces chopped bittersweet or semisweet chocolate or bittersweet chocolate chips, melted and cooled to room temperature

¼ cup unsweetened cocoa powder

1 pound mini chocolate chips (about 2 cups)

Sweetened Whipped Cream (page 59)

One 4-ounce bar or chunk semisweet chocolate, for topping

1. Position the rack in the center of the oven. Heat the oven to 350°F. Generously butter the inside of a 13 x 18-inch lipped sheet pan.

2. Mix the chocolate graham cracker crumbs, melted butter, confectioners' sugar, and milk in a large bowl until uniform and moistened. Pour and spread this mixture into the prepared pan, then use clean, dry fingers to press it into an even crust across the bottom and up the sides of the prepared sheet pan.

3. Using a handheld electric mixer or a stand mixer with the paddle attachment, beat the cream cheese and white sugar in a large bowl at medium speed until light and smooth, about 3 minutes.

4. Beat in the yogurt until smooth. Beat in the eggs one at a time, then beat in the melted chocolate and cocoa powder until evenly distributed. Scrape down and remove the beaters or paddle.

5. Using a silicone spatula, fold in the chocolate chips until evenly distributed. Pour and spread this mixture into the prepared crust.

6. Bake until puffed and set with the barest jiggle at its center when tapped, about 35 minutes. Cool in the pan on a wire rack to room temperature, about 3 hours. Cover loosely with plastic wrap and refrigerate for at least 6 hours or up to 2 days.

7. Spread the whipped cream evenly over the cheesecake. To make chocolate curls, run a vegetable peeler down the long side of the chocolate bar or across a flat surface of the chunk, letting the resulting curl fall onto the cheesecake below. Soldier on until the cake is evenly covered with the curls.

TESTER NOTES

You may not use all of the chocolate to make the curls. You need a large enough block so you can hold it steady.

WHITE CHOCOLATE CHEESECAKE WITH LEMON GLAZE

For the best flavor, look for artisanal, nondeodorized white chocolate, a product that smells and tastes a bit like dark chocolate (the aromas from the cacao beans have not been chemically removed) yet still has that characteristic, buttery texture of white chocolate. This white chocolate will have enough oomph to stand up to this sweet-sour glaze that's basically lemon curd thinned with sour cream.

For the cheesecake

Vanilla Cookie Crust (see page 117)
12 ounces chopped white chocolate or white chocolate chips
¾ cup heavy cream
2 pounds full-fat cream cheese, softened to room temperature
1 cup granulated white sugar
5 large eggs, at room temperature
2 teaspoons finely grated lemon zest plus 2 tablespoons fresh lemon juice

1. Position the rack in the center of the oven. Heat the oven to 350°F. Prepare and shape the crust as directed in a 13 x 18-inch lipped sheet pan.

2. Put the white chocolate and cream in a medium microwave-safe bowl. Microwave on high in 10-second bursts, stirring after each, until melted and smooth. Cool for 20 minutes at room temperature, stirring occasionally.

3. Using a handheld electric mixer or a stand mixer with the paddle attachment, beat the cream cheese and sugar in a large bowl at medium speed until creamy and light, about 3 minutes.

4. Beat in the eggs one at a time, then beat in the white chocolate mixture until smooth. Beat in the lemon zest and juice. Pour and scrape this mixture into the prepared crust.

5. Bake until puffed and set with a slight jiggle at its center, 30 to 35 minutes. Cool in the pan on a wire rack to room temperature, about 3 hours. Cover loosely with plastic wrap and refrigerate for at least 4 hours or up to 2 days.

For the glaze

1 cup granulated white sugar
10 tablespoons (or 1¼ sticks) unsalted butter, cut into small chunks
8 large egg yolks, at room temperature
1 tablespoon finely grated lemon zest plus ⅔ cup fresh lemon juice
1 cup full-fat or low-fat sour cream

1. Set up a double boiler or a heat-safe bowl that fits snugly over a medium saucepan with about 1 inch of slowly simmering water. Place the sugar, butter, egg yolks, lemon zest, and lemon juice in the top half of the double boiler or the bowl. Whisk constantly until thickened and glossy, 10 to 12 minutes.

2. Scrape the mixture into a medium bowl and cool to room temperature, about 1 hour, stirring occasionally. Stir in the sour cream until smooth. Spread this mixture evenly over the cheesecake.

TESTER NOTES
The easiest way to separate an egg is to crack the egg in your cupped palm, then open your fingers slightly and tilt your hand toward a medium bowl, letting the egg white run between your fingers.

BANANA PUDDING CHEESECAKE

This recipe's a bit more technical than some of the other cheesecakes in this book. You'll need a (clean!) instant-read thermometer or a laser thermometer to make sure you get the custard to the right temperature before you beat the cream cheese into it. The results are worth the mad scientist routine: an intense, creamy cross between banana pudding and cheesecake.

Animal Cracker Crust (page 117)
5 very ripe medium bananas, peeled and thinly
    sliced
7 large eggs, at room temperature
1 tablespoon vanilla extract
1 teaspoon banana flavoring or extract, optional
4½ cups whole or 2% milk
1½ cups granulated white sugar
¾ cup all-purpose flour
1 tablespoon cornstarch
½ teaspoon salt
2 pounds full-fat cream cheese, softened to
    room temperature
2 cups crumbled pecan pralines (about 8
    ounces), for topping

1. Position the rack in the center of the oven. Heat the oven to 375°F. Prepare and press the crust into a buttered 13 x 18-inch lipped sheet pan.

2. Bake for 10 minutes or just until set. Cool on a wire rack to room temperature, about 1 hour.

3. Spread the banana slices in an even layer across the crust. Whisk the eggs, vanilla, and banana flavoring, if using, in a large bowl until creamy, about 2 minutes.

4. Clean and dry the whisk. Whisk the milk, sugar, flour, cornstarch, and salt in a large saucepan set over medium heat until the mixture bubbles and thickens somewhat, about 4 minutes.

5. Whisk about half the milk mixture into the egg mixture in a thin, steady stream until smooth, then whisk this combined mixture into the remaining milk mixture in the pan.

6. Set the pan over medium-low heat and cook, stirring constantly, until the temperature registers 170°F on a clean instant-read meat thermometer or a laser kitchen thermometer. Set aside off the heat.

7. Using a handheld electric mixer or a stand mixer with the paddle attachment, beat the cream cheese in a large bowl at medium speed until light and smooth, about 2 minutes. Beat in the hot milk mixture until smooth. Gently pour this mixture over the banana slices in the crust. Refrigerate until set, at least 6 hours or up to 2 days, covering with plastic wrap once cool.

8. Before serving, pulse the pralines in a food processor until the consistency of fairly fine sand. Sprinkle this mixture over the top of the cheesecake before slicing into squares.

TESTER NOTES
Of course, you don't have to dust this cheesecake with pecan pralines. You could use any brittle you like to make the dust, even peanut brittle!

KEY LIME CHEESECAKE WITH OAT CRUMBLE

Bet you've never had a crumble topping on a cheesecake. Okay, at least not on a sheet cheesecake. Here's a tart, creamy filling between a crunchy, cookie crust that is also used to create a crumble over the cheesecake as it bakes. The results are decidedly buttery and rich, a hybrid cheesecake–slab pie concoction that would be best on a summer evening after a barbecue.

For the crumble crust and topping

24 tablespoons (3 sticks) cool unsalted butter, cut into small chunks, plus additional for the sheet pan
3½ cups all-purpose flour
3½ cups rolled oats
1½ cups granulated white sugar
1½ cups packed light brown sugar
1 tablespoon baking powder
1 teaspoon salt
1 large egg white, at room temperature

1. Generously butter the inside of a 13 x 18-inch lipped sheet pan.

2. Using a handheld mixer or a stand mixer with the paddle attachment, beat the flour, oats, both sugars, the baking powder, and the salt in a large bowl at medium speed until uniform, about 1 minute.

3. Add the butter chunks and beat at medium-low speed until well blended, about 4 minutes. Add the egg white and beat at medium speed until the mixture can hold together like a dry oatmeal cookie dough when squeezed, less than 1 minute.

4. Scoop 6 cups of this mixture into the prepared sheet pan; use clean, dry fingers to press the mixture into an even crust across the bottom (even to the corners, but not up the sides) of the pan.

For the cheesecake

1 pound full-fat cream cheese, softened to room temperature
One 14-ounce can full-fat sweetened condensed milk
1 cup fresh lime juice
½ cup granulated white sugar
6 large egg yolks, at room temperature

1. Position the rack in the center of the oven. Heat the oven to 350°F.

2. Put the cream cheese, condensed milk, lime juice, sugar, and egg yolks in a large food processor or blender. Cover and process or blend until smooth. Pour this mixture onto the prepared crust in an even layer.

3. Squeeze small portions of the remaining crumble mixture into little oblongs, then crumble these into little stones and pebble across the filling.

4. Bake until browned and set with a slight jiggle to the center of the pan, about 30 minutes. Cool in the pan on a wire rack for at least 1 hour before cutting into squares to serve.

TESTER NOTES
Refrigerating this cheesecake can make the crumble topping go boggy. Best to make it and serve it on the same day.

PEAR AND GINGER CHEESECAKE

This last cheesecake is a flight of fancy. You'll make a crust by grinding granola with vanilla wafer cookies, then you'll top it with a rich cream cheese mixture that's laced with a gingery pear compote. Use a plain granola without added fruit (although it can have nuts, if you like). You'll end up with a sophisticated set of flavors, best with a glass of aged rum and a long evening ahead.

10 dried pear halves, chopped
¼ cup chopped crystallized ginger
1 cup pear nectar
12 tablespoons (1½ sticks) unsalted butter, melted and cooled to room temperature, plus additional for the sheet pan
30 vanilla wafer cookies
2 cups plain granola
2 pounds full-fat cream cheese
½ cup packed light brown sugar
⅓ cup granulated white sugar
4 large eggs, at room temperature
⅓ cup all-purpose flour
1 tablespoon vanilla extract

1. Combine the dried pears, crystallized ginger, and pear nectar in a medium saucepan. Bring to a simmer over medium heat, stirring often. Remove from heat, cover, and set aside until all the liquid is absorbed, about 40 minutes.

2. Process the pear mixture in a food processor until smooth. Pour into a medium bowl and cool to room temperature, about 20 minutes.

3. Position the rack in the center of the oven.

Heat the oven to 350°F. Generously butter the inside of a 13 x 18-inch lipped sheet pan.

4. Clean and dry the food processor bowl and blade. Put the cookies and granola in the food processor; cover and process until coarsely ground. Add the melted butter and pulse until combined and moistened. Pour and press this mixture into the prepared sheet pan, forming an even crust across the bottom and about halfway up the sides of the pan.

5. Using a handheld electric mixer or a stand mixer with the paddle attachment, beat the cream cheese and both sugars in a large bowl at medium speed until light and fluffy, about 3 minutes. Beat in the eggs one at a time, then beat in the cooled pear puree, followed by the flour and vanilla, all until smooth. Pour and spread this mixture into the prepared crust.

6. Bake until puffed and set with the slightest jiggle at its center when tapped, 30 to 33 minutes. Cool in the pan on a wire rack to room temperature, about 1½ hours. Cover loosely with plastic wrap and refrigerate for at least 4 hours or up to 24 hours.

TESTER NOTES
Dried pears should be soft and pliable, not hard or cracked. They should definitely smell like delicate, ripe, fresh pears, neither fermented nor dusty.

THREE SIMPLE CRUSTS

These crusts are used in several cheesecake recipes here as well as others in the next two sections about slab pies. You can pretty well use any one you like for any recipe, although we always tell you what we think works best. Even better, two of them are no-bake crusts.

GRAHAM CRACKER CRUST

For a real treat, add up to 1 teaspoon salt with the graham crackers.

12 tablespoons (1½ sticks) unsalted butter, melted and cooled to room temperature, plus additional for the sheet pan
One 14.4 ounce box graham crackers, finely ground; or 4 cups graham cracker crumbs
¼ cup packed light brown sugar

1. Generously butter the inside of a 13 x 18-inch lipped sheet pan.

2. Mix the graham cracker crumbs and sugar in a medium bowl until uniform. Stir in the melted butter until moistened.

3. Pour the mixture into the prepared sheet pan. Use clean, dry fingers to press the mixture into an even crust across the bottom and up the sides of the pan.

VANILLA COOKIE CRUST

Because vanilla wafer cookies are drier than graham crackers we upped the butter in this crust.

16 tablespoons (2 sticks) unsalted butter, melted and cooled to room temperature, plus additional for the sheet pan

One 15-ounce box plus 10 extra Nilla Wafer or other vanilla wafer cookies, finely ground; or 4 cups vanilla wafer cookie crumbs
¼ cup confectioners' sugar

1. Generously butter the inside of a 13 x 18-inch lipped sheet pan.

2. Mix the cookie crumbs and confectioners' sugar in a medium bowl until uniform. Stir in the butter until moistened.

3. Pour the mixture into the prepared sheet pan. Use clean, dry fingers to press the mixture into an even crust across the bottom and up the sides of the pan.

ANIMAL CRACKER CRUST

This crust needs to be prebaked. In most cases, it will also need to cool to room temperature before you top it, even if it will then get baked again.

1 pound animal cracker cookies (about 120 cookies), finely ground
½ cup confectioners' sugar
16 tablespoons (2 sticks) unsalted butter, melted and cooled to room temperature

1. Position the rack in the center of the oven. Heat the oven to 350°F.

2. Stir the cookie crumbs and confectioners' sugar in a large bowl until uniform. Stir in the melted butter until evenly moistened.

3. Pour this mixture into a 13 x 18-inch lipped sheet pan. Use clean, dry fingers to press the crumb mixture into an even crust across the bottom and up the sides of the pan. (The sides may be a little ragged.

4. Bake for 5 minutes. Transfer to a wire rack to cool to room temperature, at least 1 hour.

CLASSIC SLAB PIES

And now for the other half of our book: slab pies, all made in that same 13 x 18-inch sheet pan, all fit for crowds, but none with any worries about the batter's crumb or structure. Instead, these are acreages of pie goodness. You're going to start rolling out crusts. Don't panic. We'll help. And the results will be worth every ounce of effort.

The Traditional Slab Pie

When old-school cooks think of a slab pie, they mostly imagine a fruit dessert. So that's where we'll start: with cherry, apple, blueberry, nectarine, peach, and more. A few of these pies are two-crust affairs: a thick, jam-like filling between two crunchy layers. But most involve innovative topping alternatives. Some get a crumble on top, about like a few of our coffee cakes and cheesecakes. Others get a bread-crumb topping, or a crunch topping like what's on top of a crisp, or a cobbler-like biscuit topping, or even a meringue over a lemony custard. You can mix and match most of these, although we wouldn't recommend putting that meringue on anything but a custard or cream pie.

Frozen Fruit

We often call for frozen fruit rather than fresh. And our recipes often ask for the fruit to remain frozen as it's folded into the filling. There are several reasons for this. Because of how it's picked, frozen fruit proves sweeter than fresh. It's also somewhat drier, allowing the filling to set up more easily. It puts most of the pies within easy reach even in the depths of winter. And it's more economical than its fresh kin.

However, there's a downside to all that good news. Frozen fruit can make a filling mixture tough to handle. When it gets stirred in, the other ingredients get so cold, they almost seize up. You'll have to work diligently, using a sturdy wooden spoon to stir it all together.

Remember, too, that frozen fruit doesn't pick up the dry ingredients as readily as sticky fresh fruit does. If you find sugar or flour left in the bowl, sprinkle the remainder evenly over the fruit filling in the sheet pan.

In fact, frozen blueberries will never bind with the dry ingredients. Make sure you've got even distribution across the big expanse of the pie.

Stock up when you see sales of frozen fruit at the supermarket. You'll be that much closer to a fruit slab pie when the hankering hits you.

Instant Tapioca

Many of these recipes call for this old-fashioned ingredient, perhaps more familiar to your grandmother than to you. Instant tapioca is not made up of standard tapioca pearls; rather, it's very coarsely ground tapioca starch that's been parcooked so it dissolves more easily. It'll yield a rich, jam-like set to the pies. Look for instant tapioca in the baking aisle of almost all North American supermarkets.

Storing Fruit Slab Pies

Fruit slab pies can remain at room temperature for up to one day without much damage to their texture or flavor. After that, they should be covered loosely with plastic wrap, then they'll hold in the refrigerator for another two days. But take note: the bottom crust will get increasingly boggy. Maybe that's a fair trade in your books. Or maybe not.

And Finally . . .

Not a one of these slab pies is as thick as a traditional pie. These recipes are for those of us who unabashedly love pie crust, for those of us who always dreamed of slathering a crisp cookie with jam. Get out your rolling pin. There's no turning back.

THE GIANT JAM SLAB

In many ways, Pop-Tarts are the spirit of slab pies. But there's one problem: they're just not big enough! So here's a giant slab tart that's got enough servings to go around (and around again). It's a great treat for an afternoon snack or even a weekend breakfast. The white icing is exceptionally sweet. You could leave it off—or put it on the side as a dip. But all that said, if you're going to get out the rolling pin for a crust, consider starting here.

5 cups all-purpose flour, plus additional for the work surface

6 tablespoons granulated white sugar

2 teaspoons salt

2 cups solid vegetable shortening

At least ¾ cup very cold water

40 ounces jam (about 4 cups), such as raspberry, blackberry, or apricot

2½ to 3 cups confectioners' sugar

⅓ cup whole or 2% milk

1 teaspoon vanilla extract

At least 2 tablespoons nonpareils, colored sprinkles, or jimmies, for topping

1. Position the rack in the center of the oven. Heat the oven to 350°F.

2. Whisk the flour, sugar, and salt in a large bowl until uniform. Cut in the shortening with a pastry cutter or a fork until the mixture resembles coarse sand, with a few bits of shortening visible.

3. Stir in ¾ cup cold water, then add more cold water in 1-tablespoon increments just until the mixture comes together into a dough. The less you fool with it, the more tender it will be.

4. Divide the dough into two balls. Cover one with a clean kitchen towel. Lightly flour a clean, dry work surface. Set the other half of the dough on it, press into a squat, 2-inch thick rectangle, and dust it with flour. Roll it into a 13 x 18-inch rectangle.

5. Use an offset spatula or a long, thin, metal blade to loosen the dough from the work surface on all sides. Gently fold it up without creasing it and transfer it to the sheet pan. Unfold and gently press it into a crust across the bottom (not the sides) of the pan. Spread the jam evenly over the crust, leaving a 1-inch border at the edges. Using a pastry brush or your clean finger, paint those edges with a little water.

6. Lightly dust the work surface again with flour. Set the second piece of dough on it and repeat that rolling operation, getting it to a slightly larger size, a little shy of 14 x 19 inches. Again, loosen it, fold it, bring it to the sheet pan, and set it on top of the jam-spread crust. Press the edges together to seal them all around.

7. Bake until lightly browned, about 25 minutes. Cool in the pan on a wire rack to room temperature, about 1½ hours.

8. Whisk 2½ cups of the confectioners' sugar, the milk, and vanilla in a large, clean, dry bowl to make a smooth, thick, but pourable frosting. Add more confectioners' sugar in 1-tablespoon increments if it needs to be thicker. Use an offset spatula to spread this mixture over the top crust. Garnish with sprinkles while the icing is still wet, if desired.

TESTER NOTES

The top crust needs to be slightly larger than the bottom one to accommodate the mound of jam underneath. Trim off any excess before sealing the edges. You can seal the edges by pressing them together with your fingers, fluting them, or even pressing the tines of a flatware fork into them.

THE GIANT FIG SLAB

You know those figgy cookies named for a certain town in Massachusetts? Here's a slab pie that does them one better because its sheer scale has increased dramatically and because the filling is stocked with lots of fruit beyond mere figs for a more sophisticated palette of flavors. We've also crafted a dough that's fairly delicate as well as a little drier to go against the sticky filling. It's more in keeping with what wraps around the filling of those cookies, but still very tasty, thanks mostly to whole-wheat flour in the mix.

1¼ pounds dried figs, preferably Turkish or white figs, stemmed and cut into small bits
18 ounces dried cranberries
2 large tart apples, such as Granny Smith, peeled, cored, and cut into small bits
1¼ cups packed light brown sugar
⅓ cup fresh lemon juice
⅓ cup fresh orange juice
⅓ cup brandy
½ teaspoon ground cinnamon
2 cups cake flour
2 cups whole-wheat flour
2 cups all-purpose flour, plus additional for dusting
1 teaspoon baking powder
1 teaspoon baking soda
1 teaspoon salt
1 cup solid vegetable shortening
6 large eggs, at room temperature, whisked until smooth

1. Position the rack in the center of the oven. Heat the oven to 350°F.

2. Put the dried figs, dried cranberries, and apples in a large food processor. Cover and pulse until the mixture is a pasty amalgam with a coarse texture, certainly not a puree. Scrape into a medium saucepan.

3. Stir in the brown sugar, lemon juice, orange juice, brandy, and cinnamon. Bring to a simmer over medium heat, stirring often. Reduce the heat a bit and continue cooking, stirring often, until thickened, about 5 minutes. Scrape into a bowl and cool to room temperature, about 1 hour.

4. Using a handheld electric mixer or a stand mixer with the paddle attachment, blend all three flours, the baking powder, baking soda, and salt at low speed in a very large bowl. Add the shortening and beat at medium speed until well combined. Pour in the eggs and continue beating until a dough forms.

5. Scrape down and remove the beaters or the paddle. Gather the dough into a compact ball; divide it in half. Set one half under a clean kitchen towel. Set the other half in a 13 x 18-inch lipped sheet pan. Use clean, dry fingers to press the dough into a crust across the

bottom of the sheet pan. Spread the dried fruit mixture evenly over the crust, leaving a ½-inch border on all sides.

6. Dust a clean, dry work surface with flour. Set the other half of the dough in the center and roll into a 13 x 19-inch rectangle. (Note the slightly longer length.) Use a flatware knife to divide the dough widthwise into 1- to 1½-inch-wide strips. Loosen these one by one and transfer them to the sheet pan, lining them up the short way across the filling so that they barely overlap. Press and join the edges of the strips to the bottom crust.

7. Bake until lightly browned and firm to the touch, about 25 minutes. Cool in the pan on a wire rack for at least 20 minutes before slicing into pieces for serving.

TESTER NOTES
If you don't want to use brandy, substitute unsweetened apple cider or increase the fresh orange juice to ⅔ cup.

SPICED PEACH PIE WITH AMARETTI CRUNCH

Spiced peach halves were a holiday necessity back in the day—and maybe still make an appearance at some of our tables, particularly for those of us who get nostalgic for "the day." They were sweet tidbits, heavily accented with warming spices like cinnamon and allspice. We've moved those flavors away from side-dish duty and morphed them into this big pie, something of a throwback but a welcome treat on a fall day when the last of the peaches are in.

For the pie

4½ pounds ripe but firm medium peaches, peeled, pitted, and thinly sliced; or 4 pounds frozen sliced peaches, thawed
1¼ cups packed light brown sugar
¼ cup all-purpose flour
¼ cup instant tapioca
2 teaspoons fresh lemon juice
1 teaspoon ground cinnamon
1 teaspoon ground dried ginger
½ teaspoon salt
¼ teaspoon freshly grated nutmeg
Single-crust version of Sour Cream Crust (page 148)

1. Position the rack in the center of the oven. Heat the oven to 350°F.

2. Mix the peaches, brown sugar, flour, tapioca, lemon juice, cinnamon, ginger, salt, and nutmeg in a large bowl until the peaches are evenly coated. Set aside for 10 minutes.

3. Meanwhile, prepare and shape the crust as directed in a 13 x 18-inch lipped sheet pan.

4. After 10 minutes, stir the filling well, then spread it evenly into the prepared crust. Do not wash the bowl.

For the amaretti crunch

1½ cups all-purpose flour
1½ cups crushed amaretti cookies
1 cup sliced almonds
1 cup granulated white sugar
12 tablespoons (1½ sticks) unsalted butter, melted and cooled to room temperature

1. Combine the flour, crushed cookies, almonds, and sugar in the bowl used for the filling. Stir in the melted butter until evenly moistened. Squeeze, crumble, and scatter this mixture in dribs and drabs across the top of the filling.

2. Bake until the topping has browned and the filling below is bubbling, about 45 minutes. Cool in the pan on a wire rack for at least 1 hour before serving.

TESTER NOTES

The most time-consuming part of this recipe is the crunchy topping—not making it, but getting it scattered over the big pie. Use that now-familiar technique from our coffee cake crumbles: squeeze small bits into lumps, then break these apart into little bits and sandy extras across the top of the filling.

APPLE PIE WITH GINGERBREAD CRUMBLE

Here's an apple slab pie without a top crust, a fairly easy treat on a fall evening—that is, after you've peeled all the fruit. (Isn't that what children are for?) The crumble topping will be best if the size of the crumbles varies dramatically, from small pellets to sandy bits, yet still covers the filling completely and evenly. After that, it's just a matter of having good vanilla ice cream on hand when the pie is still warm.

For the pie

4 pounds tart medium baking apples, such as Granny Smith or Empire, peeled, cored, and sliced (about 10½ cups)
1¼ cups granulated white sugar
¼ cup all-purpose flour
3 tablespoons instant tapioca
½ teaspoon ground cinnamon
½ teaspoon salt
Single-crust version of Shortening-Butter Crust (page 146)

1. Position the rack in the center of the oven. Heat the oven to 350°F.

2. Toss the apples, sugar, flour, tapioca, cinnamon, and salt in a large bowl until the slices are well coated and the sugar has begun to dissolve. Set aside for 10 minutes.

3. Meanwhile, prepare and shape the crust as directed in a 13 x 18-inch lipped sheet pan.

4. After 10 minutes, stir the filling before pouring and spreading it into the crust. Do not wash the bowl.

For the crumble

16 tablespoons (2 sticks) unsalted butter, melted and cooled to room temperature
2 cups packed dark brown sugar
1½ cups all-purpose flour
2 teaspoons ground dried ginger
1 teaspoon ground cinnamon
½ teaspoon freshly grated nutmeg
¼ teaspoon salt

1. Stir the melted butter, brown sugar, flour, ginger, cinnamon, nutmeg, and salt in the bowl used for the filling until the mixture is loose, moistened, but crumbly. Squeeze this mixture by small handfuls and crumble these over the top of the filling in bits and pieces anywhere from the size of small pebbles to larger, ¾-inch bits.

2. Bake until the fruit is bubbling and the topping has browned, about 50 minutes. Cool in the pan on a wire rack for at least 1 hour before serving.

APPLE-CRANBERRY PIE WITH OATMEAL COOKIE CRUMBLE

Okay, now we get more complicated. Here, you'll make one mixture that'll serve as both the crust and the crumble topping, depending on what additives you give to each and how you work with them in the recipe. It's pretty demanding, but there's bourbon in the mix to ease your troubles. By the way, since the results are pretty dramatic, avoid cheap booze. You need a good bourbon to offer maximum flavor.

24 tablespoons (3 sticks) unsalted butter, melted and cooled to room temperature, plus additional for the sheet pan

3½ pounds tart medium baking apples, such as Empire or McIntosh, peeled, cored, and diced (about 9 cups)

3½ cups plus 2 tablespoons all-purpose flour

1¾ cups granulated white sugar

¾ cup dried cranberries

3 tablespoons bourbon

3 cups rolled oats

2 cups packed light brown sugar

1 tablespoon baking powder

1 teaspoon ground cinnamon

1 teaspoon salt

¼ cup water

2 cups finely chopped walnuts

1 teaspoon vanilla extract

1. Position the rack in the center of the oven. Heat the oven to 350°F. Generously butter the inside of a 13 x 18-inch lipped sheet pan.

2. Mix the apples, 6 tablespoons of the flour, ¾ cup of the granulated white sugar, the cranber-ries, and bourbon in a large bowl until the apples are thoroughly coated. Set aside.

3. Using a handheld electric mixer or a stand mixer with the paddle attachment, mix the remaining 3¼ cups flour, the remaining 1 cup granulated white sugar, the oats, brown sugar, baking powder, cinnamon, and salt in a second large bowl at medium speed until uniform.

4. Add the melted butter and beat at low speed until the mixture forms a dry crumble that will hold together when squeezed into little bits. Scoop out one-third of this mixture, place it in a small bowl, cover with a clean kitchen towel, and set aside.

5. Stir the water into the crumbly dough remaining in the large bowl until the dough can hold its shape. Pour into the prepared pan and press this mixture evenly across the bottom with clean, dry fingers to form a crust.

6. Spoon and spread the apple mixture over the crust.

7. Stir the walnuts and vanilla into the reserved crumbly mixture. Squeeze small handfuls of this mixture into oblongs, then crumble these into small pebbles and dusty bits across the top of the filling.

8. Bake until the filling is bubbling at the edges and the topping has browned, about 1 hour. Cool in the pan on a wire rack for at least 1 hour before serving.

SWEET CHERRY PIE WITH PECAN CRUNCH

Have you ever wanted to hybridize a pie and a crisp? We did, too! So we layered a buttery crust under this sweet, cherry filling, then topped it with a mixture that might go on top of a tasty crisp. Note that we call for sweet cherries, like Bing or so-called "dark" cherries. They'll give a richer, more comforting finish to the flavors, particularly under this nutty topping. Best of all, this slab pie works best with frozen cherries, so it can be made all year long without much fuss.

For the pie

Single-crust version of All-Butter Crust
    (page 147)
4 pounds frozen pitted sweet cherries
    (do not thaw)
1⅓ cups granulated sugar
¼ cup instant tapioca
¼ cup all-purpose flour
1 tablespoon limoncello or fresh lemon juice
½ teaspoon vanilla extract
½ teaspoon salt

1. Position the rack in the center of the oven. Heat the oven to 350°F.

2. Stir the cherries, sugar, tapioca, flour, limoncello or lemon juice, vanilla, and salt in a large bowl until the cherries are evenly coated. Set aside for 10 minutes.

3. Meanwhile, prepare and shape the crust as directed in a 13 x 18-inch lipped sheet pan.

4. After 10 minutes, stir the filling, then pour and spread it into the prepared crust. Do not wash the bowl.

For the crunch

3 cups all-purpose flour
1½ cups chopped pecans
1 cup plus 2 tablespoons granulated white sugar
18 tablespoons (2¼ sticks) unsalted butter,
    melted and cooled
½ teaspoon ground cinnamon
½ teaspoon salt

1. Stir the flour, pecans, sugar, melted butter, cinnamon, and salt in the bowl used for the filling until evenly moistened but bound into a ball. Squeeze this mixture into small handfuls, then crumble these evenly over the filling in small pebbles and sandy bits.

2. Bake until the filling is bubbling and the crunch topping is golden brown, about 50 minutes. The topping may begin to brown too deeply after about 35 minutes. If so, cover loosely with aluminum foil until the filling is bubbling, then uncover and bake a couple of minutes, just to dry out the topping. Cool in the pan on a wire rack for at least 1 hour before serving.

TESTER NOTES

Old-fashioned sweet cherry pies are often made with a little almond extract. Feel free to add ½ teaspoon to the filling mixture for that classic flavor. However, if you do, do not use limoncello, only lemon juice, and reduce its amount to 1½ teaspoons.

STRAWBERRY-RHUBARB PIE

The filling for this first big two-crust pie is pretty straightforward. We're not reinventing the wheel (yet). However, a double-crust slab pie requires a lot of work to make the bottom and top slabs of dough. Still, consider this: there's a certain Zen-like bliss that can come from baking desserts for family and friends. Slow down, take your time, and enjoy the process. There's no reason to stress. There's pie in the offing.

Double-crust version of Shortening-Butter
    Crust (page 146)
2½ pounds fresh rhubarb, thinly sliced (about
    4½ cups); or 2½ pounds frozen rhubarb (do
    not thaw)
1½ pounds fresh strawberries, hulled and thinly
    sliced (about 4 cups)
1¾ cups granulated white sugar
6 tablespoons all-purpose flour
¼ cup instant tapioca
½ teaspoon salt

1. Position the rack in the center of the oven. Heat the oven to 350°F.

2. Prepare the crust as directed and shape the bottom crust in a 13 x 18-inch lipped sheet pan.

3. Toss the rhubarb, strawberries, sugar, flour, tapioca, and salt in a large bowl. Pour and spread this mixture across the crust.

4. Shape the top crust as directed, sealing the edges and cutting the vents.

5. Bake until the filling is bubbling through the slits and the crust has browned, about 50 minutes. Cool in the pan on a wire rack for at least 1 hour before cutting into squares to serve.

TESTER NOTES

If using fresh, thick rhubarb spears, consider peeling them before slicing. Start at the thicker end, nick up a little of the red coating with a paring knife, then zip the coating down the stalk. You'll loose some of the red coloring but also, more importantly, the stringy bits. You don't have to remove every bit of the red. About two-thirds gone from each stalk will work. (Frozen rhubarb slices are almost always peeled.)

STRAWBERRIES AND CREAM PIE WITH HONEY CRUMBLE

You know how good it is when you pour heavy cream over strawberries with a buttery cookie alongside? Well, you will now! Here's a creamy filling under a cookie-like topping, terrific picnic fare. And if you've got a little extra cream to pour over each serving, it'll be even better!

For the pie

Single-crust version of Shortening-Butter Crust (page 146)
3¾ pounds fresh strawberries, hulled and thinly sliced (about 11 cups)
1 cup granulated white sugar
½ cup heavy cream
½ cup all-purpose flour
¼ cup instant tapioca
1 teaspoon vanilla extract
½ teaspoon salt

1. Position the rack in the center of the oven. Heat the oven to 350°F.

2. Mix the strawberries, sugar, cream, flour, tapioca, vanilla, and salt in a large bowl until the strawberries are evenly coated in the mixture and the sugar has begun to dissolve. Set aside for 10 minutes.

3. Meanwhile, prepare and shape the crust as directed in a 13 x 18-inch lipped sheet pan.

4. Stir the filling, then spread it into an even layer in the crust. Do not wash the bowl.

For the crumble

3 cups all-purpose flour
1½ cups rolled oats
¾ cup sliced almonds
16 tablespoons (2 sticks) unsalted butter, melted and cooled to room temperature
¾ cup honey
¾ cup packed light brown sugar
½ teaspoon ground cinnamon
½ teaspoon salt

1. Stir the flour, oats, and sliced almonds in the bowl used for the filling. Add the melted butter, honey, brown sugar, cinnamon, and salt. Stir until evenly moistened. Crumble in bits and small pieces across the top of the filling.

2. Bake until the filling is bubbling and the crumble is a dark golden brown, about 50 minutes. If the crumble begins to brown too deeply before the filling is bubbling, tent the pie loosely with aluminum foil and continue baking. Remove the cover for a minute or two at the end of baking to dry out the crumble. Cool in the pan on a wire rack for at least 1 hour before serving.

TESTER NOTES
For the most intense flavor, use clover honey or even a strong, dark honey.

STRAWBERRY PIE WITH PEANUT BUTTER CRUMBLE

By mixing sliced strawberries with strawberry jam, we can create a filling that's a little sticky, even chewy, a good partner to the crunchy crumble on top of this giant slab pie. We've also created a different crust from any other in the book. It's like a big sugar cookie, a better match to the filling. Buy the sweetest, most aromatic, but still firm strawberries you can find.

For the pie
24 tablespoons (3 sticks) cool unsalted butter, cut into small chunks, plus additional for the sheet pan
1 cup packed dark brown sugar
¾ cup granulated white sugar
2 large egg whites, at room temperature
2 cups all-purpose flour
2 cups rolled oats
1 cup graham cracker crumbs
1 teaspoon ground cinnamon
1 teaspoon salt
1¼ pounds fresh strawberries, hulled and thinly sliced (about 3¼ cups)
21 ounces strawberry jam (about 2⅓ cups)

1. Position the rack in the center of the oven. Heat the oven to 350°F. Generously butter the inside of a 13 x 18-inch lipped sheet pan.

2. Using a handheld mixer or a stand mixer with the paddle attachment, beat the butter and both sugars in a large bowl at medium speed until light, creamy, and velvety, about 7 minutes. Beat in the egg whites one at a time.

3. Beat in the flour, oats, graham cracker crumbs, cinnamon, and salt until the mixture forms into moist clumps like a cookie dough.

Pour this mixture into the prepared sheet pan and press it into an even crust across the bottom.

4. Mix the strawberries and jam in a big bowl until uniform. Spread across the crust.

For the crumble
1⅓ cups rolled oats
¾ cup all-purpose flour
½ teaspoon salt
¾ cup plus 2 tablespoons natural-style crunchy peanut butter
¾ cup plus 2 tablespoons packed light brown sugar
11 tablespoons (1 stick plus 3 tablespoons) unsalted butter, softened to room temperature
2 teaspoons vanilla extract

1. Mix the oats, flour, and salt in a small bowl.

2. Using a handheld mixer or a stand mixer with the paddle attachment, beat the peanut butter, brown sugar, and butter in a large bowl at medium speed until creamy and smooth, about 3 minutes. Scrape down the inside of the bowl, then beat in the vanilla.

3. Scrape down and remove the beaters or paddle. Add the flour mixture and stir with a wooden spoon just until crumbly and uniform. Crumble this mixture evenly over the filling.

4. Bake until bubbling and browned, about 45 minutes. Cool in the pan on a wire rack for at least 1 hour before serving.

BLUEBERRY-ORANGE PIE

Okay, yes, another double-cruster among our offerings. This one's got an unbeatable combo: blueberries and a little orange to set off the sweetness. If you don't want the alcohol in the filling, substitute the same amount of fresh-squeezed orange juice. Other than that, just take your time rolling out the crust, making sure you loosen it from the surface time and again to make sure it's not sticking. At the end of it all, you'll also need vanilla ice cream. Trust us.

Double-crust version of Shortening-Butter Crust
  (page 146)
3 pounds frozen blueberries (do not thaw)
1⅓ cups granulated white sugar
¼ cup orange-flavored liqueur, such as Blue
  Curaçao or triple sec
¼ cup all-purpose flour
3 tablespoons instant tapioca
2 teaspoons finely grated orange zest
½ teaspoon ground cinnamon
½ teaspoon salt

1. Position the rack in the center of the oven. Heat the oven to 350°F.

2. Prepare the crust as directed and shape the bottom crust in a 13 x 18-inch lipped sheet pan.

3. Mix the blueberries, sugar, orange liqueur, flour, tapioca, zest, cinnamon, and salt in a large bowl. Pour and spread this mixture evenly into the crust. Set aside for 10 minutes.

4. Shape the top crust as directed, sealing the edges and cutting the slits.

5. Bake until the filling is bubbling through the slits and the crust has lightly browned, about 50 minutes. Cool in the pan on a wire rack for at least 1 hour before slicing into squares to serve.

TESTER NOTES
This filling actually tastes better with frozen blueberries. They're picked closer to ripeness and then flash-frozen, often right in the field, so they're sweeter and stocked with juice. (The fresh ones are often picked earlier and allowed to ripen a bit on their way to market.)

MIXED-BERRY PIE

Here's another double-crust pie that works best with frozen fruit. The berries won't turn to jam as the filling bakes. And let's face it: frozen berries are more economical. That said, if you want to use fresh berries, you'll need about 3½ pounds (hull and slice any strawberries) We've topped the pie with a lattice crust. It's beautiful, yes; but more importantly, it allows for more evaporation during baking to help the filling set properly.

4 pounds mixed frozen berries, any strawberries sliced into ½-inch pieces (do not thaw)
1½ cups granulated white sugar
¼ cup all-purpose flour, plus additional for dusting
¼ cup instant tapioca
1 teaspoon vanilla extract
½ teaspoon ground cinnamon
½ teaspoon salt
Double-crust version of Sour Cream Crust (page 148) or All-Butter Crust (page 147)

1. Position the rack in the center of the oven. Heat the oven to 350°F.

2. Mix the berries, sugar, flour, tapioca, vanilla, cinnamon, and salt in a big bowl. Set aside while you roll out the crust.

3. Prepare the crust as directed and shape the bottom crust in a 13 x 18-inch lipped sheet pan.

4. Pour and scrape every drop of the berry mixture into the prepared crust, creating a filling with an even depth across its surface.

5. Roll out the smaller portion of the dough as directed. However, do not move it to the sheet pan. Instead, loosen it from the work surface with an offset spatula, then use a fluted pastry roller or just a flatware knife to cut the dough sheet lengthwise into ½-inch-wide strips (be careful of your counter below). Lay these in alternating directions over the filling, trimming half to make them fit the short way over the filling and thereby creating a lattice top to the pie. Slice off some of the excess dough at the edges and seal the lattice strips to the crust sticking up at the edge.

6. Bake until the filling is bubbling and the crust is golden brown, about 50 minutes. If the crust begins to brown too deeply, tent the pie loosely with aluminum foil and continue to bake until bubbling. Remove the foil for the last couple of minutes so that the crust dries out a bit. Cool in the pan on a wire rack for at least 1 hour before serving.

NECTARINE-BLUEBERRY PIE WITH WALNUT CRUNCH

Here's summer in a slice. But there's no way this rather simple slab pie will taste right if you don't use good nectarines. The only secret is your nose. If the nectarines don't smell like anything, they won't taste like anything. The topping is quite rich, loaded with nuts. It'll work best if they're in very small bits, not sandy, but certainly nothing more than about ¼ inch long.

For the pie

10 ripe medium nectarines, peeled, pitted, and sliced (about 8 cups)
10 ounces fresh blueberries (about 2 cups)
¾ cup granulated white sugar
½ cup packed light brown sugar
6 tablespoons all-purpose flour
3 tablespoons instant tapioca
2 tablespoons dark rum, such as Myers's
½ teaspoon salt
Single-crust version of Shortening-Butter Crust (page 146)

1. Position the rack in the center of the oven. Heat the oven to 350°F.

2. Mix the nectarines, blueberries, both sugars, flour, tapioca, rum, and salt in a large bowl until the fruit is evenly coated. Set aside for 10 minutes.

3. Meanwhile, prepare and shape the crust as directed in a 13 x 18-inch lipped sheet pan.

4. Stir the filling, then pour and spread it evenly into the prepared crust. Do not wash the bowl.

For the crunch

2 cups all-purpose flour
1 cup rolled oats
10 tablespoons (1¼ sticks) unsalted butter, melted and cooled to room temperature
½ cup honey
½ cup packed dark brown sugar
½ cup finely chopped walnuts
1½ teaspoons ground cinnamon
½ teaspoon salt

1. Mix the flour, oats, melted butter, honey, dark brown sugar, walnuts, cinnamon, and salt in the bowl used for the filling. Stir until the mixture is moistened but doesn't necessarily hold together. Squeeze small handfuls of this mixture into oblongs, then crumble and scatter them over the filling in varying sizes of pebbles and dust.

2. Bake until the fruit filling is bubbling and the topping has browned, about 45 minutes. Cool in the pan on a wire rack for at least 1 hour before serving.

PEAR PIE WITH BREAD-CRUMB CRUNCH

Consider this our homage to the Brown Betty, a classic American dessert of sweetened, sliced fruit baked among and under buttery bread crumbs. We've spread the filling out into a slab pie, then topped it with the bread crumbs, so that they don't go soggy as quickly as they do in the traditional version. Some slab pies can be "hand desserts," served on a napkin at an outdoor picnic. Not this one. You'll need forks and plates.

For the pie

10 ripe, medium Bartlett pears, stemmed, peeled, cored, and thinly sliced (about 8 cups)
1½ cups granulated white sugar
¼ cup all-purpose flour
¼ cup instant tapioca
1 teaspoon ground dried ginger
½ teaspoon salt
Single-crust version of All-Butter Crust (page 147)

1. Position the rack in the center of the oven. Heat the oven to 350°F.

2. Mix the pears, sugar, flour, tapioca, ginger, and salt in a large bowl until the pear slices are evenly coated. Set aside for 10 minutes.

3. Meanwhile, prepare and shape the crust as directed in a 13 x 18-inch lipped sheet pan.

4. Stir the mixture, then spread it into the prepared crust. Do not wash the bowl.

For the crunch

5 cups fresh bread crumbs
1 cup pine nuts, finely chopped
10 tablespoons (or 1¼ sticks) unsalted butter, melted and cooled to room temperature
½ cup packed light brown sugar
½ teaspoon freshly grated nutmeg

1. Mix the bread crumbs, pine nuts, melted butter, brown sugar, and nutmeg in the bowl used for the filling until evenly moistened and uniform. Squeeze it into lumps and crumble these into very small bits and sandy leftovers across the top of the filling.

2. Bake until the topping is lightly browned and the filling is bubbling, about 45 minutes. If the topping begins to brown too deeply, cover the pan loosely with aluminum foil but uncover it for the last couple of minutes of baking so the topping dries out. Cool in the pan on a wire rack for at least 1 hour before serving.

TESTER NOTES

The best crumbs for this topping are four or five plain hamburger buns (no seeds or flavorings), cut into chunks, frozen, and ground in the food processor.

RASPBERRY-ALMOND COBBLER PIE

Man, that recipe title sounds like bureaucrat speak, a lot of nouns pounded up against each other! But it's a necessary evil to explain this hybrid, a jam-like raspberry filling between a bottom pie crust and a somewhat traditional biscuit topping. In any event, it's a summery treat (even in the winter, since you make it with frozen raspberries). Make sure the cobbler topping is evenly spaced across the top of the pie so the cut pieces each come out with some biscuit on top.

2 cups sliced almonds
Single-crust version of Sour Cream Crust (page 148)
4 pounds frozen raspberries (do not thaw)
2¼ cups plus 3 tablespoons all-purpose flour
2 cups plus 1 tablespoon granulated white sugar
¼ cup instant tapioca
2 teaspoons finely minced lemon zest
1½ teaspoons salt
4½ teaspoons baking powder
1½ cups regular cultured buttermilk
6 tablespoons (¾ stick) unsalted butter, melted and cooled to room temperature
½ teaspoon almond extract

1. Position the rack in the center of the oven. Heat the oven to 350°F.

2. Spread the sliced almonds on a large lipped sheet pan. Toast until lightly browned and fragrant, stirring occasionally, about 5 minutes. Put the nuts in a food processor and cool for 20 minutes. Maintain the oven's temperature.

3. Cover and process the toasted almonds into a fine flour.

4. Prepare and shape the crust as directed in a 13 x 18-inch lipped sheet pan.

5. Mix the raspberries, 3 tablespoons of the flour, 1½ cups of the sugar, the tapioca, lemon zest, and 1 teaspoon salt in a large bowl. Pour and spread into an even layer in the prepared crust.

6. Whisk the ground almonds, the remaining 2¼ cups flour, the remaining ½ cup plus 1 tablespoon sugar, the remaining ½ teaspoon salt, and the baking powder in a medium bowl until uniform. Stir in the buttermilk, melted butter, and almond extract just until combined. Dollop this mixture by rounded tablespoonfuls over the raspberry filling, spacing the blobs evenly apart.

7. Bake until the filling is bubbling and the topping is golden brown, about 50 minutes. Cool in the pan on a wire rack for at least 1 hour before serving.

TESTER NOTES
Don't start dolloping the biscuit topping on one end of the sheet pan to work your way across. You might find out you run out of biscuits! Instead, cover the whole pie with ten, maybe twelve dollops, then start filling in the spaces between them.

LEMON BUTTERMILK PIE

To get a sweet-and-sour blend that can't be beat, this slab pie needs to ripen in the fridge. To get the proper texture of firm, somewhat chewy pudding, make sure you get the right set in the oven: a little wiggling at the center, not liquid, but not fully firm. When you tap the corner of the pan (with an oven-mitted hand!), you should see some movement at the pie's center, nothing dramatic, no waves or even ripples, but just some definite jiggle.

Single-crust version of Shortening-Butter Crust
    (page 146)
2 cups granulated white sugar
6 large eggs, at room temperature
3 cups regular cultured buttermilk
16 tablespoons (2 sticks) unsalted butter, melted
    and cooled to room temperature
4½ teaspoons finely grated lemon zest plus 3
    tablespoons fresh lemon juice
2 tablespoons cornstarch
1 teaspoon lemon extract, optional
¼ teaspoon salt
½ teaspoon freshly grated nutmeg

1. Position the rack in the center of the oven. Heat the oven to 350°F.

2. Prepare and shape the crust as directed in a 13 x 18-inch lipped sheet pan. Prick the crust repeatedly with a flatware fork across the flat surface and up the sides. Cover loosely with aluminum foil and bake for 20 minutes. Uncover and set on a wire rack while you prepare the filling. Maintain the oven's temperature.

3. Using a handheld electric mixer or a stand mixer with the whisk attachment, beat the sugar and eggs in a large bowl at medium speed, until thick and rich, about 6 minutes. Beat in the buttermilk, melted butter, lemon zest and juice, cornstarch, lemon extract (if using), and salt until smooth. Pour into the prebaked crust. Dust the top with the grated nutmeg.

4. Bake until lightly browned and the pie has a slight jiggle at the center, about 30 minutes. Cool in the pan on a wire rack to room temperature, about 1 hour. Cover loosely with plastic wrap and store in the refrigerator for at least 6 hours or up to 2 days before serving.

LEMON MERINGUE PIE

Here's a classic American pie morphed into a big slab. One warning: it won't keep. Meringue pies rarely do. The topping eventually weeps as the crust goes soggy under the filling. But the confectioners' sugar will help stabilize the meringue a little longer than traditional ones made with granulated white sugar.

Single-crust version of Shortening-Butter Crust
(page 146)
6 large eggs, separated, plus 6 large egg whites,
at room temperature
1 teaspoon salt
2 cups granulated white sugar
1¾ cups water
One 15-ounce can evaporated whole milk
1 cup fresh lemon juice
¾ cup cornstarch
2 teaspoons lemon extract
½ teaspoon cream of tartar
1⅔ cups confectioners' sugar
2 teaspoons vanilla extract

1. Position the rack in the center of the oven. Heat the oven to 350°F.

2. Prepare and shape the crust as directed in a 13 x 18-inch lipped sheet pan. Prick the crust repeatedly with a flatware fork across the flat surface and up the sides. Cover loosely with aluminum foil and bake for 20 minutes. Uncover and continue baking until lightly browned, about 5 minutes. Use a flatware fork to prick any parts of the crust that bubble up. Transfer to a wire rack. Increase the oven's temperature to 400°F.

3. Whisk the six egg yolks and ½ teaspoon of the salt in a large bowl until creamy and smooth, about 2 minutes.

4. Clean and dry the whisk. Whisk the sugar, water, evaporated milk, lemon juice, cornstarch, and lemon extract in a large saucepan set over medium heat until the sugar dissolves. Continue cooking, whisking constantly, until somewhat thickened and bubbling without boiling, about 8 minutes.

5. Whisk about half the sugar mixture into the egg yolk mixture in a slow, steady stream. Then whisk this combined mixture into the remaining sugar mixture in the saucepan until smooth. Pour and spread this filling into the crust.

6. While the filling is still hot, use an electric mixer or a stand mixer with the whisk attachment to beat the twelve egg whites in a large bowl at low speed until foamy. Add the cream of tartar and the remaining ½ teaspoon salt; increase the speed to high and beat until you can make soft, droopy peaks.

7. Beat in the confectioners' sugar in 2-tablespoon increments until the mixture is thick and can hold its shape in firm peaks on the turned-off beaters. Beat in the vanilla. Spread this mixture evenly over the hot pie filling. Seal it well against every single bit of the crust all around the pan. Using a silicone spatula, make wavy peaks and valleys in the meringue.

8. Bake only until the meringue is light brown, about 7 minutes. Cool in the pan on a wire rack for at least 1½ hours, then refrigerate for at least 1 hour or up to 8 hours before serving.

THREE TRADITIONAL CRUSTS FOR
SLAB PIES AND CHEESECAKES

These recipes all require a good rolling technique. And be forewarned: the crusts are massive. In any event, here are the rules of engagement:

1. Use only as much flour as necessary. More will lead to tougher crusts.

2. Handle the crust mixture as little as possible. Repeatedly messing with it can stretch the gluten and toughen the crust.

3. Smush the crust dough into a rectangle under your clean, dry palm before you begin to roll it out, so you're not trying to "square" a circle.

4. Roll from the middle to the edge, repositioning the rolling pin each time.

5. Invest in a fairly lightweight wooden rolling pin. Don't let the pin exert force through its sheer weight. Rather, you should exert a light but firm pressure on the pin for a more even crust.

SHORTENING-BUTTER CRUST

A combination of shortening and butter makes a sturdier crust with just a hint of buttery flavor. Make sure that the butter is still cold from the fridge and that the water used to pull the dough together is quite cold, even ice water, to keep the fat chilled until it hits the oven. As a make-ahead boon, you can prepare, roll out, and shape a single crust of this dough in the sheet pan, then cover it loosely with clean kitchen towels and store it in the fridge for up to four hours. Set it out on the counter as you prepare the filling to remove a little of the chill.

For a Single Crust

4 cups all-purpose flour, plus additional for dusting
½ teaspoon salt
1⅓ cups solid vegetable shortening
4 tablespoons (½ stick) cold unsalted butter, cut into small chunks
At least ¾ cup very cold water

1. Mix the flour and salt in a large bowl, then cut in the shortening and butter with a flatware fork or a pastry cutter until the mixture resembles coarse sand, working the mixture repeatedly through the tines to get the desired consistency.

2. Stir in ¾ cup cold water, then add more in 1-teaspoon increments, until the mass coheres into a fairly dry, certainly not sticky, dough. Gather the dough into a ball.

3. Dust a clean, dry work surface with flour and set the ball of dough on it. Use your clean, dry palm to squash the dough into a 2-inch-thick rectangle. Dust it with flour and roll it into a 16 x 21-inch rectangle.

4. Loosen the edges of the dough from the work surface with an offset spatula or a long, thin metal blade, then fold the dough once or twice for transport. Move it to a 13 x 18-inch lipped sheet pan. Unfold the dough and press it into an even crust across the bottom and up the sides of the pan. Flute the edges as desired or simply trim off any excess.

For a Double Crust

7 cups all-purpose flour, plus additional for dusting
¾ teaspoon salt
2⅓ cups solid vegetable shortening
7 tablespoons cool unsalted butter, cut into small chunks
At least 1⅓ cups very cold water

1. Complete steps 1 and 2 as above with the larger quantities of ingredients, adding more cold water as necessary in 1-tablespoon increments.

2. Divide the dough in half. Wrap one half in plastic wrap and store in the fridge until you're ready for it. Roll out the other half as described in steps 3 and 4 above. However, when you get it into the sheet pan as an even crust, do not trim off the overhanging excess.

3. Once the filling is in the pan, clean and dry the work surface, dust it with flour, and roll the second ball of dough as you did the first. However, this time make a 15 x 20-inch rectangle.

4. Transfer it to the sheet pan as before, then open it up over the filling. Crimp and seal the two crusts together. If desired, ornament the edges. Cut several vents in the top crust.

TESTER NOTES

Any leaking filling will be on your head. If desired, decorate the edges by repeatedly pressing the tines of a flatware fork into the sealed perimeter or flute it by placing the thumb and forefinger of one hand on the inside rim and pushing the forefinger of the other hand into that "U" (repeat all the way around the crust). When you cut several vents in the top crust, consider a decorative pattern. Geometric? Your initials? A couple of traced strawberries? Just remember: you're not making cut-outs. The lines shouldn't meet up but simply give the outline of the pattern.

ALL-BUTTER CRUST

We find that a little sugar in an all-butter crust mellows it a tad and gives it a bit more "crunch." We also add a little acid here, just enough to inhibit a little gluten formation to keep the crust "shorter"—crunchier, with more flaky goodness. This amount of acid won't change the pH of the dough much. After all, we do want gluten structure for the crust. But it provides just enough oomph that the results will be impossibly light with zillions of layers.

For a Single Crust

4 cups all-purpose flour, plus additional for dusting
1 tablespoon granulated white sugar
1 teaspoon salt
24 tablespoons (3 sticks) cold unsalted butter, cut into small chunks
At least ¾ cup very cold water
1 teaspoon fresh lemon juice

1. Mix the flour, sugar, and salt in a large bowl, then cut in the butter with a flatware fork or a pastry cutter until the mixture resembles coarse sand, working the mixture repeatedly though the tines to get the desired consistency.

2. Stir in ¾ cup cold water and the lemon juice, then add more water in 1-teaspoon increments, until the mass coheres into a fairly dry, certainly not sticky, dough. Gather the dough into a ball, wrap it tightly in plastic wrap, and refrigerate for at least 45 minutes or up to 4 hours.

3. Dust a clean, dry work surface with flour and set the ball of dough on it. Squash the dough into a 2-inch-thick rectangle. Dust it with flour and roll it into a 16 x 21-inch rectangle.

4. Loosen the edges of the dough from the work surface with an offset spatula or a thin, long, metal blade, then fold the dough once or twice for transport. Move it to a 13 x 18-inch lipped sheet pan. Unfold the dough and press it into an even crust across the bottom and up the sides of the pan. Flute the edges as desired or simply trim off any excess.

For a Double Crust

7 cups all-purpose flour
5 teaspoons granulated white sugar
1½ teaspoons salt
43 tablespoons (5 sticks plus 3 tablespoons) cold unsalted butter, cut into small chunks
At least 1⅓ cups very cold water
1½ teaspoons fresh lemon juice

1. Mix the flour, sugar, and salt in a large bowl, then cut in the butter with a flatware fork or a pastry cutter until the mixture resembles coarse sand, working the mixture repeatedly though the tines to get the desired consistency.

2. Stir in 1⅓ cups cold water and the lemon juice, then add more water in 1-tablespoon increments, until the mass coheres into a fairly dry, certainly not sticky, dough. Gather the dough into a ball and divide it in half. Wrap each half tightly in plastic wrap and refrigerate for at least 45 minutes or up to 4 hours.

3. Dust a clean, dry work surface with flour and set one piece of dough on it. Squash the dough into a 2-inch-thick rectangle. Dust it with flour and roll it into a 16 x 21-inch rectangle.

4. Loosen the edges of the dough from the work surface, then fold the dough once or twice for transport. Move it to a 13 x 18-inch lipped sheet pan. Unfold the dough and press it into an even crust across the bottom and up the sides of the pan. Don't trim the excess.

5. Once the filling is in the pan, clean and dry the work surface, dust it with flour, and roll the second ball of dough as you did the first. However, this time make a 15 x 20-inch rectangle.

6. Transfer it to the sheet pan as before, then open it up over the filling. Crimp and seal the two crusts together. If desired, ornament the edges. Cut several vents in the top crust.

SOUR CREAM CRUST

This crust is the richest in the lot, best under cream fillings or dried fruit pies. It's also a bit sticky, so it rolls out better if it's had a chance to rest in the fridge. Do not use low-fat or fat-free sour cream. You'll need all the fat to form the flakiness. But okay, yes, the double-crust recipe calls for seven sticks of butter. Look for sales and store butter in your freezer for up to one year. In that case, let the butter come to room temperature for ten or fifteen minutes before you begin to work with it.

For a Single Crust

4 cups all-purpose flour, plus additional for dusting
4½ teaspoons granulated white sugar
2 teaspoons salt
32 tablespoons (4 sticks) cool unsalted butter, cut into small chunks
1 cup full-fat sour cream, cold from the refrigerator

1. Whisk the flour, sugar, and salt in a large bowl until uniform. Cut the butter into the mixture with a flatware fork or a pastry cutter until the whole thing looks like coarse grit with some slightly smaller bits throughout.

2. Stir in the sour cream until moist dough coheres in the bowl. Gather it into a ball, wrap it tightly in plastic wrap, and store in the refrigerator for at least 1 hour or up to 4 hours.

3. Unwrap the dough and set aside at room temperature for 10 minutes.

4. Dust a clean, dry work surface with flour, set the dough on top of it, and squash it into a 2-inch-thick rectangle. Dust it with flour and roll into a 16 x 21-inch rectangle. Be precise! To work the edges properly, roll from the center out, working in long, even strokes. Even up the edges with a ruler and then continue to roll until you get it to the right size.

5. Loosen the dough from the work surface, fold it into halves or thirds without creasing it, and transfer it to a 13 x 18-inch lipped sheet pan. Unfold the dough and press it into an even crust across the bottom and up the sides of the pan. Trim off any excess.

For a Double Crust

7 cups all-purpose flour, plus additional for dusting
7½ teaspoons granulated white sugar
1 tablespoon salt
56 tablespoons (7 sticks) cool unsalted butter, cut into chunks
1¾ cups full-fat sour cream, cold from the refrigerator

1. Follow the directions for the single crust but with the larger amounts of the ingredients from step 1 through 3, except divide the dough in half, form each into a ball, and wrap each separately in plastic wrap before refrigerating.

2. Roll one ball into a 16 x 21-inch rectangle, following the instructions in step 4 above. When you unfold and press it into the sheet pan, do not trim off the excess.

3. Once the filling is in the pie, clean and dry the work surface. Dust it with flour, unwrap the second ball of dough, and set it in the center. Squash it into that squat rectangle, dust it with flour, and roll it into a 15 x 20-inch rectangle. Loosen it from the work surface, fold gently without any creases, and unfold it on top of the filled pie.

4. Crimp and seal the two crusts together. If desired, flute the edges. Cut several vents in the top crust, perhaps in a decorative pattern.

CHOCOLATE SLAB PIES

& Other Favorites

Now things get richer—and a little more complicated. Many of the fruit slab pie recipes in the last section just asked you to stir together some basic ingredients and bake them in the crust. But these recipes include icebox pies, custard pies, and nut pies, all a little more labor-intensive. And the final two in this batch, both dried fruit pies, are unabashed showstoppers that require a bit of effort. Stock up on the ingredients. No doubt about it, you're going to use a lot.

Storing the Pies

Most cream and custard slab pies go right into the refrigerator so the filling can set up. Make sure you have enough room in your fridge for a giant tray of pie. Check by fitting the sheet pan on a shelf before you start.

All of these pies can stay put in the fridge for up to two days, provided they're loosely covered with plastic wrap. (But beware: the crust will get a little soggy after twenty-four hours.) Sadly, none freezes well.

All that said, these pies taste better when they're not cold from the fridge. If you've made one in advance, leave it out on the counter for fifteen to twenty minutes before serving.

Chocolate

Pay particular attention to the type of chocolate in each recipe. If we call for dark chocolate and you use semisweet, the pie can become cloyingly sweet.

In general, dark chocolate has 70 to 75 percent cocoa solids in the mix. Bittersweet has 60 to 65 percent; and semisweet, 45 to 55 percent. Yes, it's best to skip any labeling and buy chocolate by the percentage of cocoa solids in the mix. But we've kept the window dressing of "dark," "bittersweet," and such in our ingredient lists because it's still the American standard way to describe chocolate. That said, you can customize up and down in the percentages to create the taste and finish you prefer. Just don't get a recipe that calls for dark chocolate too sweet by using semisweet chips.

Nuts

Shelled nuts go rancid quickly at room temperature, sometimes in a month or so in warm climates. Improve their shelf life by storing them in sealed, opaque containers in the refrigerator for up to nine months or in the freezer for up to two years. Always smell and taste-test nuts before you use them. There's no point in wasting effort on a pie if it's not going to taste good.

Gluten-Free Crusts

Most of these pies call for one of the three crusts in the previous section (pages 146–149). However, you can make a gluten-free crust. Rather than buying the individual components, search out gluten-free pie crust mixes, sold in most large supermarkets and at many online outlets. In general, we find that we can get a single crust for a 13 x 18-inch sheet pan by using *two* 16-ounce bags of gluten-free pie crust mix. (Thus, you'll need four bags for a double crust pie.) Follow the recipe on the bags to prepare the crust.

And So . . .

Perhaps more than any other recipes in this book, these are things of patience. They require accuracy and planning. Don't shortchange the steps; don't rush them by upping the temperature under a pot. You have to settle in and relax. That's not a bad thing at all, given the usual pace of our modern world.

FRENCH SILK CHOCOLATE PIE

We start our chocolate pies with something of an American classic (despite its name). French silk pie came to prominence in the 1950s, a rich dessert befitting the burgeoning prosperity after World War II. Our version is fully cooked, no raw eggs in the mix as is sometimes traditional. In a better bid for safety, we can still craft a velvety-smooth pie.

Single-crust version of All-Butter Crust (page 147)
1 pound dark chocolate, preferably 70% cocoa solids, chopped
2 cups heavy cream
6 large eggs, at room temperature
1½ cups granulated white sugar
¼ cup chocolate liqueur, such as crème de cacao
1 tablespoon vanilla extract
16 tablespoons (2 sticks) unsalted butter, softened to room temperature
Sweetened Whipped Cream (page 59)

1. Position the rack in the center of the oven. Heat the oven to 350°F.

2. Prepare and shape the crust as directed in a 13 x 18-inch lipped sheet pan. Prick the crust repeatedly with a flatware fork across the flat surface and up the sides.

3. Cover loosely with foil, then bake for 20 minutes. Uncover and continue baking until light brown and set, about 10 minutes. Cool in the pan on a wire rack to room temperature, about 1 hour.

4. As the crust cools, heat the chocolate in a small bowl in the microwave oven, giving it 10-second bursts on high and stirring after each, until about three-quarters melted. Remove the (hot!) bowl from the microwave and continue stirring until smooth. Cool to room temperature, about 20 minutes, stirring occasionally.

5. Using a handheld electric mixer or a stand mixer with the whisk attachment, beat the cream in a large bowl at high speed until you can make soft peaks. Remove the beaters or whisk and set the bowl in the refrigerator. If using a handheld mixer, clean and dry the beaters.

6. Set up a double boiler or a heat-safe bowl that fits snugly over a medium saucepan with about 1 inch of slowly simmering water. Put the eggs, sugar, liqueur, and vanilla in the top half of the double boiler or the bowl. Using a handheld mixer at medium speed or a whisk, beat the egg mixture over the barely simmering water until thick, pale yellow, and fluffy, about 10 minutes.

7. Remove the top half of the double boiler or the bowl from the heat. Continue beating or whisking at medium speed until room temperature, about 10 minutes.

8. Beat in the melted chocolate until smooth. Scrape down the inside of the bowl, then beat in the butter 1 tablespoon at a time.

9. Scrape down and remove the beaters. Fold in the whipped cream with a silicone spatula until evenly distributed, using wide, gentle arcs to get it incorporated without deflating it too much.

10. Spread and smooth this chocolate mixture into the cooled pie crust. Refrigerate for at least 4 hours or up to 2 days, covering the pie loosely with plastic wrap once it's cold.

11. To serve, smooth and spread the sweetened whipped cream over the pie. Or get fancy and pipe it in lines, stars, or rosettes over the pie.

TESTER NOTES

For a chocolate coffee flavor, substitute espresso or very strong coffee for the chocolate liqueur.

CHOCOLATE WALNUT PIE

Consider this dessert a chocolate lover's answer to a nut pie. The filling is fudgy and dense because there's no flour or cornstarch in the mix. If you don't care for walnuts, feel free to substitute pecans or even hazelnuts. By the way, don't fear the corn syrup. It's gotten a lot of bad press and no, you don't want to use it every day. But it's the only way to get that classic, sort of jelly-like set to a nut pie.

Single-crust version of Shortening-Butter Crust (page 146)
14 tablespoons (1¾ sticks) unsalted butter, cut into chunks
2 ounces unsweetened chocolate, chopped
8 large eggs, at room temperature
1 cup packed dark brown sugar
1 cup dark corn syrup
½ cup unsweetened cocoa powder
1 tablespoon vanilla extract
1 teaspoon salt
1¼ pounds walnuts, chopped (about 4 cups)

1. Position the rack in the center of the oven. Heat the oven to 350°F.

2. Prepare and shape the crust as directed in a 13 x 18-inch lipped sheet pan. Prick the crust repeatedly with a flatware fork across the flat surface and up the sides.

3. Loosely cover the crust with aluminum foil. Bake for 10 minutes. Transfer to a wire rack, remove the foil, and cool while you prepare the filling. Maintain the oven's temperature.

4. Melt the butter and chocolate in a large saucepan set over medium-low heat, stirring almost all the while, until about two-thirds of the chocolate has melted. Remove from the heat and continue stirring until smooth. Set aside to cool for 15 minutes.

5. Whisk in the eggs one at a time, then whisk in the brown sugar and corn syrup until smooth. Whisk in the cocoa powder, vanilla, and salt. Finally, stir in the walnuts and pour into the crust.

6. Bake until puffed and set, and until the center jiggles slightly when the sides of the pan are tapped, about 40 minutes. Cool in the pan on a wire rack for at least 1 hour before serving.

TESTER NOTES

More than any other recipe in this book, this one *requires* that the eggs be at room temperature. If they're cool, they'll slow down the baking and cause the edges of the pie to get overdone, a little dry and cracked. By the way, if you substitute a gluten-free pie-crust mix, this slab pie becomes a gluten-free treat.

CHOCOLATE CUSTARD PIE

This one's a fairly simple chocolate custard pie that gets poured over lots of chocolate chips set on the crust. Everything rests on the quality of those chips. Don't cheap out. Use a high-quality brand without shortening or other fillers. The crust is only partially set at first because it will also be baked under the filling. However, the crust must be thoroughly cooled in step 3 so it doesn't melt the chips.

Single-crust version of Shortening-Butter Crust
    (page 146)
12 tablespoons (1½ sticks) unsalted butter, cut
    into small chunks
3 ounces unsweetened chocolate, chopped
12 ounces bittersweet or dark chocolate chips
    (about 2 cups)
3 cups packed dark brown sugar
2¼ cups evaporated whole milk
6 large eggs plus 3 large egg yolks, at room
    temperature
2 tablespoons vanilla extract
½ teaspoon salt
¾ cup all-purpose flour, plus additional for
    dusting
¾ cup unsweetened cocoa powder

1. Position the rack in the center of the oven. Heat the oven to 350°F.

2. Prepare and shape the crust as directed in a 13 x 18-inch lipped sheet pan. Prick the crust repeatedly with a flatware fork across the flat surface and up the sides.

3. Cover it loosely with aluminum foil. Bake for 10 minutes. Transfer to a wire rack, remove the foil, and cool to room temperature, about 30 minutes. Maintain the oven's temperature.

4. As the crust cools, warm the butter and unsweetened chocolate in a large saucepan set over medium-low heat, stirring quite often, until about two-thirds of the chocolate has melted. Remove from the heat and continue stirring until all the chocolate has melted. Cool to room temperature, about 30 minutes.

5. Once the crust has cooled, scatter the chocolate chips across it in an even layer.

6. Whisk the brown sugar into the melted chocolate mixture until smooth, then whisk in the evaporated milk, eggs, egg yolks, vanilla, and salt until uniform. Add the flour and cocoa powder; whisk just until combined. Pour and scrape this batter over the chocolate chips without dislodging them.

7. Bake until puffed and set, 28 to 30 minutes. Cool in the pan for at least 1 hour before serving.

TESTER NOTES
On several occasions, we've doubled the salt in the mix for a salty finish to the filling. In that case, we've only used dark chocolate chips.

RUN FOR THE ROSES PIE

During the Kentucky Derby, a version of this bourbon-laced, nut-filled pie is served up in the stands, a sweet treat to salve those betting losses. It's got a somewhat crackly crust on top, a little crunch over the rich filling. You'll also be astounded how much this pie smells like bourbon! Use good stuff—not the $60 bottle from the holidays, but certainly a bourbon you'd drink on the porch while you count your winnings.

Single-crust version of Shortening-Butter Crust
(page 146)
5 large eggs plus 1 large egg yolk, at room
temperature
1 cup granulated white sugar
1 cup packed dark brown sugar
6 tablespoons dark corn syrup
24 tablespoons (3 sticks) unsalted butter,
softened to room temperature
⅔ cup bourbon
15 ounces semisweet or bittersweet chocolate
chips (about 2½ cups)
9 ounces walnut pieces (about 1½ cups)
1 cup plus 2 tablespoons all-purpose flour
5 ounces pecan pieces (about 1 cup)
½ teaspoon salt

1. Position the rack in the center of the oven. Heat the oven to 350°F.

2. Prepare and shape the crust as directed in a 13 x 18-inch lipped sheet pan. Prick the crust repeatedly with a flatware fork across the flat surface and up the sides.

3. Loosely cover the crust with aluminum foil. Bake for 10 minutes. Transfer to a wire rack, remove the foil, and cool while you prepare the filling. Maintain the oven's temperature.

4. Using a handheld electric mixer or a stand mixer with the whisk attachment, beat the eggs, egg yolk, both sugars, and corn syrup in a large bowl at medium speed until you can make wide ribbons, about 7 minutes.

5. Scrape down the inside of the bowl, then beat in the butter 2 tablespoons at a time. Beat in the bourbon until smooth and uniform.

6. Turn off the mixer; add the chocolate chips, walnuts, flour, pecans, and salt. Beat at low speed until uniform with no dry specks of flour. Pour and spread into the crust.

7. Bake until golden brown and set, about 30 minutes. Cool in the pan on a wire rack for at least 1 hour before serving.

TESTER NOTES
Buy pecan pieces, rather than chopping whole pecan halves by hand, which can lead to too many tiny bits and grainy remains. You want fairly hefty chunks throughout the pie.

CHOCOLATE AND COFFEE ICEBOX PIE

This is our take on an old-fashioned icebox pie, a light custard filling with whipped cream on top, here made even better (in our opinion) with the addition of a little coffee liqueur to balance the chocolate notes. The whole thing tastes as if your Southern grandmother made tiramisu. Okay, that doesn't make any sense. But it's still delicious.

Single-crust version of Shortening-Butter Crust (page 146)
8 ounces unsweetened chocolate, chopped
7 ounces chopped semisweet chocolate or semisweet chocolate chips
7 large egg yolks
½ teaspoon salt
5¾ cups whole milk
2½ cups granulated white sugar
⅔ cup cornstarch
½ cup coffee-flavored liqueur, such as Kahlúa, or nonalcoholic coffee syrup
Sweetened Whipped Cream (page 59)
One 2-ounce block semisweet chocolate, for topping
Instant espresso powder, for topping

1. Position the rack in the center of the oven. Heat the oven to 350°F.

2. Prepare and shape the crust as directed in a 13 x 18-inch lipped sheet pan. Prick the crust repeatedly with a flatware fork across the flat surface and up the sides.

3. Loosely cover the crust with aluminum foil. Bake for 20 minutes. Uncover and continue baking until golden brown and crisp, about 10 minutes. Transfer to a wire rack and cool to room temperature, about 1 hour.

4. Set up a double boiler or a heat-safe bowl set over a medium saucepan with about 1 inch of just barely simmering water. Put both chocolates in the top of the double boiler or the bowl and stir until about two-thirds melted. Remove the top half of the double boiler or the bowl from the heat and continue stirring until smooth. Cool at room temperature for 20 minutes, stirring occasionally.

5. Whisk the egg yolks and salt in a large bowl until smooth and creamy.

6. Whisk the milk, sugar, cornstarch, and liqueur in a large saucepan over medium heat until thickened and bubbling, about 8 minutes. Whisking all the while, slowly add about half the hot milk mixture to the egg yolk mixture until smooth. Then whisk this combined mixture into the remaining milk mixture in the pan.

7. Whisk in the melted chocolate until uniform. Pour this mixture into the baked crust and refrigerate until set, for at least 6 hours or up to 2 days, covering with plastic wrap once chilled.

8. To serve, spread the sweetened whipped cream over the pie. If desired, use a vegetable peeler to shave curls off the chocolate block, letting them fall onto the whipped cream. Dust the whipped cream with instant espresso powder.

TESTER NOTES
You can substitute strong black coffee for the liqueur. Use only ⅓ cup, increase the milk to 6 cups, and increase the sugar to 2¾ cups.

JACK AND COKE FUDGE PIE

This whiskey-and-Coke fandango is so chewy, dense, and rich, it'll actually need the whipped cream to lighten it up. No, you don't have to use Jack Daniel's. It just seems as if you should. Certainly don't use a fancy single malt. A blended whiskey will be fine, a nice depth of flavor. And one more thing: all the whiskey doesn't "cook out" of the filling. Don't kid yourself. This one's for the adults who can partake.

Single-crust version of Shortening-Butter Crust (page 146)
1½ pounds semisweet or bittersweet chocolate, chopped
11 tablespoons (1 stick plus 3 tablespoons) unsalted butter, cut into chunks
¾ cup whiskey, preferably Jack Daniel's, plus additional as needed
⅔ cup cola (do not use diet soda)
2 cups granulated white sugar
10 large eggs, at room temperature
1 tablespoon vanilla extract
1 teaspoon salt
⅔ cup all-purpose flour
1½ cups dark chocolate chunks
2 cups jarred caramel or butterscotch caramel ice cream topping
Sweetened Whipped Cream (see page 59)

1. Position the rack in the center of the oven. Heat the oven to 350°F.

2. Prepare and shape the crust as directed in a 13 x 18-inch lipped sheet pan. Prick the crust repeatedly with a flatware fork across the flat surface and up the sides.

3. Cover the crust with aluminum foil, pressing down gently to cover the exposed surface without smushing into the crust. Bake for 10 minutes. Transfer to a wire rack and remove the foil. Maintain the oven's temperature.

4. Put the chocolate, butter, whiskey, and cola in a large saucepan over medium heat. Cook, stirring constantly, until about two-thirds of the chocolate has melted. Remove from the heat and continue stirring until smooth. Pour and scrape into a large bowl; cool to room temperature, about 30 minutes.

5. Using a handheld electric mixer or a stand mixer with the paddle attachment, beat the sugar into the chocolate mixture at medium speed until smooth and light, about 3 minutes. Beat in the eggs one at a time, then beat in the vanilla and salt until uniform.

6. Scrape down the inside of the bowl. Beat in the flour just until there are no dry specks anywhere. Scrape down and remove the beaters or paddle.

7. Use a silicone spatula to fold in the chocolate chunks. Pour and spread this batter into the prepared crust.

8. Bake until puffed and set, about 25 minutes. Cool in the pan on a wire rack until room temperature, about 1½ hours.

9. Whisk the caramel in a small bowl with just enough whiskey to create a sauce that can be drizzled off the tines of a flatware fork. Smooth the sweetened whipped cream over the top of the pie. Drizzle the caramel mixture over the cake before serving.

BROWNED BUTTER CHESS PIE

Calm down. We don't want to start any food wars. Yes, there are about as many versions of chess pie in the South as there are cooks. So we aren't daring to claim authenticity. In fact, we bet there aren't too many versions made with browned butter like ours. We even left out the lemon, often the flavoring in this custard-like pie, so that the browned butter could offer its nutty notes unimpeded, a great contrast to the sour accents in the buttermilk and vinegar.

16 tablespoons (2 sticks) unsalted butter, cut into small pieces
Single-Crust version of Shortening-Butter Crust (page 146)
2 cups granulated white sugar
1 cup packed light brown sugar
6 large eggs, at room temperature
½ cup all-purpose flour
½ cup yellow cornmeal
1 teaspoon salt
1½ cups regular cultured buttermilk
2 tablespoons plain white vinegar
2 teaspoons vanilla extract
Sweetened whipped cream (see page 59), for topping

1. Position the rack in the center of the oven. Heat the oven to 350°F.

2. Melt the butter in a small saucepan set over medium-low heat. Continue cooking until a light amber brown, about 2 minutes. Remove from the heat and cool to room temperature, about 1 hour. (The butter will continue to brown and darken.)

3. Meanwhile, prepare and shape the crust as directed in a 13 x 18-inch lipped sheet pan. Prick the crust repeatedly with a flatware fork across the flat surface and up the sides.

4. Loosely cover the crust with aluminum foil and bake for 20 minutes. Set on a wire rack and uncover. (Maintain the oven's temperature.)

5. Whisk both sugars and eggs in a large bowl until smooth and creamy. Then whisk in the flour, cornmeal, and salt until dissolved. Finally, whisk in the browned butter and all the milk solids in the saucepan, as well as the buttermilk, vinegar, and vanilla, until smooth. Pour into the still-warm crust.

6. Bake until puffed, lightly browned, and almost set with just a little jiggle at the center, 25 to 28 minutes. Cool in the pan on a wire rack to room temperature, about 1½ hours; then cover with plastic wrap and refrigerate for at least 4 hours or up to 2 days before serving. Garnish individual servings with sweetened whipped cream, if desired.

COCONUT CUSTARD PIE

This rich slab pie couldn't be simpler, just right for family reunions or holiday get-togethers. You don't have to add the toppings—that is, the melted chocolate and chopped candied ginger— as we suggest. You can go more straightforward with just the rich custard. But we do think those garnishes give the pie a little elegance, an unusual twist among the more standard flavors.

Single-crust version of All-Butter Crust
   (page 147)
3 cups full-fat coconut milk
1 cup half-and-half
1 cup packed light brown sugar
8 large eggs, at room temperature
2 tablespoons vanilla extract
½ teaspoon salt
2 cups unsweetened coconut flakes
4 ounces bittersweet or semisweet chocolate,
   chopped, melted, and cooled to room
   temperature
½ cup finely minced crystallized ginger

1. Position the rack in the center of the oven. Heat the oven to 350°F.

2. Prepare and shape the crust as directed in a 13 x 18-inch lipped sheet pan. Prick the crust repeatedly with a flatware fork across the flat surface and up the sides.

3. Cover loosely with aluminum foil and bake for 20 minutes. Set on a wire rack and uncover. Maintain the oven's temperature.

4. While the crust is warm, put the coconut milk, half-and-half, brown sugar, eggs, vanilla, and salt in a very large blender or food proces-

sor. Cover and blend or process until smooth. Add the coconut and pulse just to combine. Pour this mixture into the crust.

5. Bake until the center of the custard barely jiggles when the sheet pan is tapped, about 20 minutes. Cool in the pan on a wire rack to room temperature, about 1 hour.

6. Before serving, drizzle the melted chocolate over the top of the pie and sprinkle with the chopped ginger.

BURNT SUGAR PIE

Here's an old-time Southern treat, a cream pie filling made from caramelized sugar, rich in egg yolks. It's a bit complicated to construct since you have to caramelize the sugar for the filling while also making a pie custard—which then becomes slightly bitter with that "burnt" sugar. But the flavor is quite elegant, if not necessarily a favorite among the third-grade set.

Single-crust version of Shortening-Butter Crust
   (page 146)
6 large eggs, separated, plus 6 large egg whites,
   at room temperature
5⅓ cups whole or 2% milk
1 teaspoon salt
4 cups granulated white sugar
½ cup cornstarch
¼ cup all-purpose flour
2 tablespoons unsalted butter
4 teaspoons vanilla extract
½ teaspoon cream of tartar
1⅔ cups confectioners' sugar

1. Position the rack in the center of the oven. Heat the oven to 350°F.

2. Prepare and shape the crust as directed in a 13 x 18-inch lipped sheet pan. Prick the crust repeatedly with a flatware fork across the flat surface and up the sides.

3. Loosely cover the crust with aluminum foil and bake for 20 minutes. Uncover and continue baking until lightly browned, about 5 minutes. Use a flatware fork to prick any parts of the crust that bubble up. Transfer to a wire rack to cool while you make the filling. Increase the oven's temperature to 400°F.

4. Whisk the six egg yolks in a large bowl until fairly uniform. Whisk in ⅔ cup of the milk and the salt until smooth. Finally, whisk in 1 cup of the sugar, the cornstarch, and flour until dissolved.

5. Pour the remaining 4⅔ cups milk into a large saucepan and set it over medium heat until small bubbles fizz around the inside perimeter of the pan. Reduce the heat so the milk stays this hot without coming to a simmer.

6. Pour the remaining 3 cups sugar into a heavy, large skillet. Set it over medium-high heat and cook undisturbed until the sugar is about halfway melted. Stir well, then continue cooking until caramel brown, stirring a few more times.

7. Increase the heat under the milk to medium-high. In a thin, steady stream, whisk the hot sugar syrup into the milk. Be careful: the mixture will roil and froth. Once all the syrup has been added, reduce the heat to medium and continue whisking until all the syrup has again dissolved and the mixture calms down.

Do not let the milk come to a boil again. Remove the saucepan from the heat.

8. Whisk about half this hot milk mixture into the egg yolks in a thin, steady stream until uniform. Then whisk this combined mixture back into the milk mixture in the saucepan. Set it again over medium-low heat and cook, whisking almost constantly, until thickened and bubbly, about 4 minutes. Stir in the butter and vanilla; pour the caramel mixture evenly into the prepared crust.

9. While the filling is still hot, use a handheld beater or a stand mixer with the whisk attachment to beat the twelve egg whites and the cream of tartar in a large bowl at low speed until foamy, then at high speed until you can make soft peaks. Beat in the confectioners' sugar in 1-tablespoon increments and continue beating until the mixture is glossy and you can form stiff peaks. Spread it evenly over the hot filling, sealing it carefully to the edges and filling in any cracks that appear. Use a silicone spatula to make peaks and valleys across the meringue.

10. Bake until lightly browned, about 5 minutes. Cool in the pan on a wire rack to room temperature, about 1 hour, then refrigerate for at least 1 hour or up to 6 hours before serving.

COFFEE CREAM ICEBOX PIE

We tamed the slightly bitter finish of this coffee pie with a chewy, cakey chocolate crust that ends up being about half the height of the pie. It starts out sort of like a brownie batter, so you'll need to work with an offset spatula to get it spread evenly in the sheet pan. No hills or valleys, please!

16 tablespoons (2 sticks) unsalted butter, cut into chunks, plus additional for the sheet pan
8 ounces chopped semisweet chocolate or semisweet chocolate chips
2½ cups plus 2 tablespoons granulated white sugar
8 large eggs plus 1 large egg yolk, at room temperature
2 teaspoons vanilla extract
1¼ cups plus 2 tablespoons all-purpose flour, sifted
4 cups whole milk
2 tablespoons instant coffee powder
3 tablespoons cornstarch
½ teaspoon salt
Sweetened Whipped Cream (page 59)

1. Position the rack in the center of the oven. Heat the oven to 350°F. Generously butter the inside of a 13 x 18-inch lipped sheet pan.

2. Melt the butter and chocolate in a medium saucepan set over medium-low heat, stirring until about two-thirds of the mixture is melted. Remove the pan from the heat and continuing stirring until smooth. Pour into a large bowl and cool at room temperature for 20 minutes, stirring occasionally.

3. Whisk in 1½ cups of the sugar until dissolved, then whisk in 4 of the eggs, one a time, followed by the vanilla. Remove the whisk and use a wooden spoon to stir in 1 cup of the flour, forming a fairly thick batter. Using an offset spatula, spread the batter evenly into the prepared pan.

4. Bake until puffed and set to the touch, about 20 minutes. Cool in the pan on a wire rack to room temperature, about 1 hour. Turn off the oven.

5. Mix the milk and instant coffee in a large saucepan, then set the pan over medium heat and warm until small bubbles fizz around the inside perimeter of the pan. Reduce the heat to keep the milk mixture warm without simmering.

6. Using an handheld electric mixer, beat the remaining 4 eggs, the egg yolk, and the remaining 1 cup plus 2 tablespoons sugar in a large bowl at medium speed until you can make wide ribbons, about 5 minutes. Beat in the remaining 6 tablespoons flour, the cornstarch, and the salt until smooth.

7. Beating at medium speed all the while, add about half the hot milk mixture in a thin, steady stream until smooth, then beat this combined mixture back into the remaining milk mixture in the pan. Set it over medium-low heat and cook, stirring constantly, until thickened and just beginning to bubble, about 2 minutes.

8. Spread the mixture evenly into the cooled browned crust. Set in the refrigerator and chill for at least 6 hours or up to 2 days, covering lightly with plastic wrap once cool. Cover or even pipe the top of the pie with the sweetened whipped cream or dollop some on individual pieces before serving.

TESTER NOTES

For a more intense flavor, substitute instant espresso powder for the instant coffee powder. And be careful of the mixer's electrical cord around the heating element when you beat the combined mixtures in the saucepan.

BUTTERED RUM ICEBOX PIE

Here's a somewhat more elaborate version of a vanilla icebox pie, the filling tweaked with rum and butter so that the whole thing's a decadent treat. Note that the recipe calls for aged rum, not gold or dark rum. Aged rum will give the filling oaky, complex notes. That said, if you just want to make a standard vanilla cream pie, omit the rum, use 5⅔ cups whole milk, and increase the butter to ½ cup plus 3 tablespoons (or 1 stick plus 3 tablespoons). In any event, you'll need to start the recipe early in the day (or even the day before) since the pie needs to set up in the refrigerator.

Animal Cracker Crust (page 117)
8 large egg yolks, at room temperature
2 cups granulated white sugar
½ cup cornstarch
¼ cup all-purpose flour
5 cups whole milk
⅔ cup aged rum, such as Bacardi Reserva
8 tablespoons (1 stick) unsalted butter, cut into
     small chunks
Sweetened whipped cream (page 59)

1. Prepare, shape, and bake the crust as directed in a 13 x 18-inch lipped sheet pan.

2. Whisk the egg yolks in a large bowl until smooth. Clean and dry the whisk.

3. Whisk the sugar, cornstarch, and flour in a large saucepan until uniform. Set the pan over medium heat and whisk in the milk in a steady stream; continue whisking until the sugar dissolves. Continue cooking, whisking quite often, until fairly thickened and just beginning to bubble, about 7 minutes.

4. Whisk about half of this mixture into the egg yolks in a slow, steady stream until smooth. Then whisk the combined, thick mixture into the remaining milk mixture in the saucepan. Set over medium-low heat and cook, whisking constantly, until just beginning to bubble again, 1 to 2 minutes.

5. Remove the pan from the heat. Whisk in the rum until smooth, then whisk in the butter, chunk by chunk, until melted and smooth. Pour into the prepared crust. Refrigerate for at least 6 hours before serving, covering loosely with plastic wrap once chilled. Top the pie with the sweetened whipped cream just before cutting into squares to serve.

TESTER NOTES
For a prettier finish, pipe the sweetened whipped cream onto the pie. Use a pastry bag and an open star #16 or #18 tip or a #46 basket weave tip. Or put the whipped cream in a large zipper-lock plastic bag, seal it, snip off one corner, and squeeze out lines of the whipped cream all over the pie.

PUMPKIN CRUNCH PIE

If you've got crowds this holiday, you need this recipe. Being crunch fanatics, we've always thought pumpkin pies were just too darn soft. So rather than putting a top crust on the pie or just letting it go as a plain unadorned pumpkin filling (heaven forfend!), we've added a pecan-laced topping that fuses to the filling below, giving that creamy pumpkin concoction some great crunch. You're on your own for the ice cream. (Did we mention we have some terrific choices in our book À La Mode?)

For the crust

3 cups all-purpose flour, plus additional for dusting
1 tablespoon granulated white sugar
1 teaspoon salt
16 tablespoons (2 sticks) cold unsalted butter, cut into small chunks, plus additional for the sheet pan
1 large egg (cold from the refrigerator), whisked until smooth
At least ½ cup very cold water

1. Position the rack in the center of the oven. Heat the oven to 350°F.

2. Whisk the flour, sugar, and salt in a large bowl until uniform. Cut in the butter chunks with a pastry cutter or a flatware fork until the mixture resembles coarse, white sand with almost no butter bits visible.

3. Stir in the egg until combined, then add the water and stir with a flatware fork until the mixture comes together as a soft dough, adding more water in 1-tablespoon increments as necessary.

4. Scrape this crust mixture into the prepared pan. Using clean, dry fingers, press it into a fairly even crust across the bottom and up the sides.

For the filling

Two 15-ounce cans solid-pack pumpkin
6 large eggs, at room temperature
1 cup pineapple jam
1 cup evaporated whole milk
¾ cup granulated white sugar
2 tablespoons cornstarch
1 teaspoon ground cinnamon
1 teaspoon ground dried ginger
½ teaspoon freshly grated nutmeg
½ teaspoon ground cloves
½ teaspoon salt

Put the pumpkin, eggs, pineapple jam, evaporated milk, sugar, cornstarch, cinnamon, ginger, nutmeg, cloves, and salt in a large blender. Cover and blend until smooth. Pour this mixture into the prepared crust.

For the topping

1 cup rolled oats
1 cup chopped pecans
1 cup packed light brown sugar
½ cup all-purpose flour
8 tablespoons (1 stick) unsalted butter, melted and cooled a few minutes

1. Mix the oats, pecans, brown sugar, flour, and melted butter in a medium bowl to make a loose, sandy amalgam. Gather it together by small handfuls, squeeze these together, then crumble them evenly over the filling in small pebbles and slightly larger chunks. (Don't just sand or dust it!)

2. Bake until the filling is set and the topping is lightly browned, about 35 more minutes. Cool on a wire rack for at least 1 hour before serving.

TESTER NOTES
Make sure you use solid-pack canned pumpkin, not pumpkin pie filling.

SWEET POTATO PIE

Here's a dessert version of a favorite holiday side-dish casserole in the South. No, we never much cared for it with turkey or roast beef. With all those marshmallows, it's just too sweet. But as a dessert, it's another matter entirely. We already said we were crunch fanatics. We didn't mention a certain passion for gooey, the kind you get when you melt marshmallows.

Graham Cracker Crust (page 117)
Three 15-ounce cans sweet potatoes or yams, in syrup, drained
2 cups full-fat sour cream
2 cups packed light brown sugar
8 tablespoons (1 stick) unsalted butter, melted and cooled to room temperature
4 large eggs plus 4 large egg yolks, at room temperature
2 teaspoons vanilla extract
1 teaspoon ground cinnamon
4 cups mini marshmallows

1. Position the rack in the center of the oven. Heat the oven to 350°F. Prepare and shape the crust as directed in a 13 x 18-inch lipped sheet pan.

2. Put the sweet potatoes, sour cream, brown sugar, melted butter, eggs, egg yolks, vanilla, and cinnamon in a large food processor. Cover and process until smooth, scraping down the inside of the canister at least once. Pour this mixture into the prepared crust.

3. Bake until puffed and almost set, and until the center of the pie is just a tad jiggly when the pan is tapped, about 30 minutes. Transfer to a wire rack. Maintain the oven's temperature.

4. Spread the mini marshmallows evenly over the pie. Set it back in the oven and bake just until they begin to run together, about 5 minutes. Transfer to a wire rack and cool for at least 1 hour before serving.

TESTER NOTES
There's no need to brown the marshmallows deeply. They should form a sticky, chewy topping.

BRANDIED DATE AND PECAN PIE

This is definitely not the standard pecan pie! For one thing, it's less sweet. For another, it has a richer texture, thanks to those dates soaked in brandy. They also give the filling a slightly chewier feel, so there's very little of that depressingly squishy texture that's so prevalent in pecan pies. And as for the nuts themselves, well, we felt we should have just enough filling to hold them in place. It's mostly nuts all the way down to the crust, a ridiculous extravagance.

10 ounces pitted dates
½ cup brandy
Single-crust version of Shortening-Butter Crust (page 146)
7 large eggs, at room temperature
2 cups light corn syrup
⅔ cup granulated white sugar
⅔ cup packed light brown sugar
1 tablespoon vanilla extract
½ teaspoon salt
8 tablespoons (1 stick) unsalted butter, melted and cooled to room temperature
1¾ pounds pecans, roughly chopped (about 6 cups)

1. Stir the dates and brandy in a small bowl. Set aside at room temperature for 2 hours.

2. Position the rack in the center of the oven. Heat the oven to 350°F. Prepare and shape the crust as directed in a 13 x 18-inch lipped sheet pan.

3. Pour the dates and brandy into a large blender. Add the eggs, corn syrup, both sugars, vanilla, and salt. Cover and pulse just until blended like a puree, not foamy. Add the melted butter, cover, and pulse again until blended. Pour this mixture into a large bowl. Stir in the pecans. Pour into the prepared crust.

4. Bake until puffed and almost set with a slight jiggle at the center of the pan when the side is tapped, about 35 minutes. Cool in the pan on a wire rack for at least 1 hour before serving.

TESTER NOTES
There's no need for expensive dates like Medjools or Baris. Instead, look for standard pitted dates—but certainly not the little bits of chopped, baking dates sold in boxes or pouches. Make sure to check the dates; although they claim to be pitted, every once in a while one isn't.

HOLIDAY DRIED FRUIT PIE

Without a doubt, this vies with the Fig and Date Cake (page 73) as the most intense offering in this collection. This one requires copious amounts of just about everything. Stock your pantry and you'll end up with a true treat. The bottom crust is something like a hamantasch or perhaps a thick sugar cookie. The top crust can be cut into whatever shapes you like: circles, leaves, hearts, you name it. Be an art director. Make it beautiful.

At least 3⅓ cups all-purpose flour, plus
    additional for dusting
1 teaspoon salt
½ teaspoon baking powder

1½ cups solid vegetable shortening
¾ cup granulated white sugar
3 large eggs plus 2 large egg yolks and 1 large
    egg white, at room temperature
4½ teaspoons vanilla extract
12 ounces dried apricots, preferably California
    dried apricots (about 2 cups)
12 ounces golden raisins (about 2 cups)
12 ounces pitted prunes (about 2 cups)
10 ounces pitted dates (about 2 cups)
1½ cups packed light brown sugar
8 ounces candied orange rind, chopped (about
    1 cup)
4 ounces pecan halves (about 1 cup)
8 tablespoons (1 stick) unsalted butter, melted
    and cooled to room temperature

1 teaspoon ground cinnamon
Single-crust version of Shortening-Butter Crust
   (page 146), prepared but not rolled out

1. Position the rack in the center of the oven. Heat the oven to 350°F. Whisk 3⅓ cups flour, ½ teaspoon of the salt, and the baking powder in a medium bowl until uniform.

2. Using a handheld electric mixer or a stand mixer with the paddle attachment, beat the shortening and white sugar in a large bowl at medium speed until creamy, light, and fluffy, about 5 minutes. Beat in 1 egg until well combined, then 1 egg white as well as 1½ teaspoons of the vanilla.

3. Turn off the mixer, add the flour mixture, and beat at low speed to form a crumbly yet homogenous dough. Add more flour in 1-tablespoon increments until the dough is crumbly without being a solid mass. Dump this dough-like mixture into a 13 x 18-inch lipped sheet pan. Use clean, dry fingers to press it into an even crust across the bottom and up the sides of the pan. Refrigerate for 1 hour.

4. Meanwhile, place the dried apricots, raisins, prunes, and dates in a large saucepan. Add enough water so that the fruit is submerged by 1 inch. Bring to a boil over high heat. Cover, reduce the heat to low, and simmer for 5 minutes. Drain in a colander set in the sink and cool for 15 minutes, stirring occasionally.

5. Working in batches as necessary, process the cooked fruit with the brown sugar, candied orange rind, pecans, melted butter, and cinnamon, as well as the remaining 2 eggs, 2 egg yolks, 1 tablespoon vanilla extract, and ½ teaspoon salt, in a food processor. If you've

worked in batches, stir them together into a puree in a large bowl when you're done. Spread this mixture over the chilled crust.

6. Lightly dust a dry work surface with flour. Roll the prepared crust into a sheet about ¼ inch thick. Use cookie cutters, biscuit cutters, or even a sturdy drinking glass to cut the sheet into whatever shapes you desire. Arrange and even overlap these across the filling.

7. Bake until the crust is golden brown and the filling is set, about 40 minutes. Cool in the pan on a wire rack for at least 1 hour before serving.

TESTER NOTES
If you dump the crust mixture evenly across the sheet pan, it's easier to press it into a single crust, rather than having to expand from one spot to cover the pan. If you want to cheat, you can buy two pre-made pie crusts, unroll them, and cut them into the desired shapes for the top of the pie.

SHEET STRUDEL, DANISH, SHORTBREAD

& More

There's nothing standard or traditional about these last recipes. Yes, they're all still sheet cakes or slab pies, if sometimes in spirit, rather than fact. There's a buttery, crunchy shortbread here, a baklava-like dessert, and a slab version of a traditional, crunchy dacquoise (dah-KWAHZ) with a super-rich, chocolate, French buttercream. What do they have in common? That sheet pan, of course, and the ability to serve crowds.

Working with Phyllo Dough

The standard North American package of phyllo dough has two packets of 9 x 13-inch parchment paper–like sheets. You'll need to use two of these sheets (set long side against long side) to create one layer in a 13 x 18-inch sheet pan. That said, there are some high-end brands that indeed come in 13 x 18-inch sheets. As a boon, the 13 x 18-inch sheets tend to be slightly thicker so they don't dry out and shard as quickly. Follow the package instructions for thawing any package of phyllo.

Never panic. Open one packet at a time. Clean and dry a place on your work surface (we often use a large cutting board). Unwrap the sheets and lay them out flat. Cover them with a clean, dry kitchen towel. And keep them covered as you continue with the recipe.

Fortunately, none of these desserts is so

delicate that you need to hurry up for fear of ruining the phyllo. And since you'll often work with coconut oil spray, you needn't worry about the sheets' tearing under a pastry brush. Besides, if a few sheets dry out and break apart, just piece them back together to form a single layer. However, save back a couple of perfect sheets for the top of the dessert, keeping those covered so they don't dry out until you're ready for them.

Working with Puff Pastry

Most standard supermarket brands are made with hydrogenated fat and come two sheets to a 17.3-ounce box. The recipes that follow were all developed and tested with these brands. However, there are artisanal brands available at high-end supermarkets. These usually offer one larger square sheet in each

14-ounce package. You'll need to cut the square into two rectangles and roll each to a slightly smaller size before it begins to get overworked, about 11 x 17 inches—in which case you may also have some filling left over from the recipe. These high-end brands are also about triple the price, made with butter, and feature a more traditionally "laminated" dough with many, many more layers per inch. (The standard North American varieties tend to be cakier when they bake up.)

Puff pastry dough suffers from a type of Goldilocks syndrome: it must be neither too hot nor too cold when you roll it out. If it's too cold, it will break. If it's too warm, it will mush. Instead, it should be cool to the touch while still being firm. You should not be able to put your finger through it.

Puff pastry is particularly prone to freezer burn in self-defrosting freezers. As the temperature fluctuates to get rid of frost build-up, the fat in the pastry freezes and thaws, creating little clumps of doughy toughness that prove hard to roll out. If you see a great deal of frost on the outside of a package, find another in the supermarket's case or take your business elsewhere. Follow the package instructions for thawing the pastry.

To roll out puff pastry, use more flour that you might imagine to dust both a clean, dry work surface and the dough sheet. Roll from the center out, keeping the pastry's basic, rectangular shape as you expand it to the proper size. It will shrink back a bit as you roll it. Don't worry—just keep at it. Flip it over at least once to make sure it's not sticking and dust it again with flour. And get it to an approximation of the correct size, rather than the strict sizes required for pie crusts in this book. The puff pastry will shrink a bit as it bakes, no matter how perfectly you roll it.

And Finally . . .

These are the last desserts in a book about delightful excess. We wish you many celebrations in the years ahead, many times when you're surrounded by enough people to warrant a sheet cake, a slab pie, or even one of our stranger curiosities. They often say that life is for the living. True enough. And the living are for each other.

APPLE STRUDEL

No rolling, folding, or shaping—there's hardly an easier recipe for strudel. You simply lay the phyllo sheets across the sheet pan and build up the layers by spraying them with coconut oil. Sure, you can substitute regular nonstick spray (just not baking spray). But remember: the standard spray adds no flavor. The coconut oil gives the strudel a nutty, rich finish, quite delicious with the apples.

One 5-ounce can coconut oil spray
9 large tart baking apples, such as Granny Smith
    or Empire, peeled, cored, and thinly sliced
1 cup raisins
¾ cup granulated white sugar
1 tablespoon ground cinnamon
½ teaspoon salt
½ cup plain dried bread crumbs
½ cup sliced almonds
½ cup packed dark brown sugar
One 1-pound box frozen phyllo sheets, thawed

1. Position the rack in the center of the oven. Heat the oven to 350°F. Lightly coat the inside of a 13 x 18-inch lipped sheet pan with coconut oil spray.

2. Mix the apples, raisins, white sugar, cinnamon, and salt in a large bowl until the apple slices are well coated.

3. In a second bowl, mix the bread crumbs, almonds, and brown sugar until uniform.

4. Unwrap the phyllo sheets, lay them on a clean, dry work surface, and cover them with a clean kitchen towel. Take two phyllo sheets and use them to cover the bottom of the prepared sheet pan. Spray them lightly with coconut oil, then sprinkle 2 tablespoons of the bread-crumb mixture evenly across the whole expanse. Repeat this process 11 more times, making 12 layers in the pan, each sprinkled with the bread-crumb mixture.

5. Spread the apple mixture over the top, making as even and uniform a layer as you can. Then go back to the phyllo sheet–coconut oil spray–bread-crumb mixture process, repeating it over and over until you've used up all the phyllo and all but 2 tablespoons of the bread-crumb mixture. Spray the top of the stack with coconut oil, then sprinkle it with the remaining bread-crumb mixture.

6. Bake for 25 minutes, then cover loosely with aluminum foil to keep the phyllo from browning too deeply. Continue baking until the fruit is bubbling around the edges, about 15 more minutes. Uncover and bake for 2 minutes to make sure the phyllo is crisp and golden. Cool in the pan on a wire rack for at least 45 minutes before serving.

TESTER NOTES
A strudel does not keep well: the filling starts to turn the bottom layers soggy and refrigeration signals the death knell to all its crunch. Plan on serving this one within eight hours of making it. Once it has cooled to room temperature, lay plastic wrap gently on top and pray for a dry day.

PEACH MELBA TURNOVER

This is a great treat on a fall evening. The only trick is getting the puff pastry rolled to the correct dimensions. Follow the instructions carefully, a matter more of patience than of technique. But at least there's no "turning over" to this turnover. You don't have to fold the puff pastry over the filling. It's one big slab of dessert!

12 ounces frozen raspberries (about 2½ cups)
12 ounces frozen peach slices, roughly chopped (about 2 cups)
½ cup granulated white sugar
6 tablespoons water
½ teaspoon almond extract
½ teaspoon salt
2 tablespoons cornstarch
All-purpose flour, for dusting
One 17.3-ounce box frozen puff pastry (2 sheets), thawed
1 large egg

1. Mix the raspberries, peaches, sugar, 2 tablespoons of the water, the almond extract, and salt in a medium saucepan and bring to a simmer over medium-high heat, stirring often. Reduce the heat to low and cook, stirring quite often, until the mixture is bubbling and the peaches are tender, about 5 minutes.

2. Whisk the cornstarch into 2 tablespoons of the water in a small bowl until smooth. Stir this slurry into the fruit mixture and continue cooking, stirring constantly, until thickened, about 1 minute. Cool to room temperature, about 1 hour.

3. Position the rack in the center of the oven. Heat the oven to 400°F.

4. Dust a clean, dry work surface with flour. Set one sheet of puff pastry in its middle, then dust it generously with flour. Roll the pastry into a 13 x 18-inch rectangle, turning it over once to make sure it's loose and pliable and dusting it with more flour as necessary. Transfer it to a 13 x 18-inch lipped sheet pan. Spread the fruit mixture evenly over the top, leaving a ½-inch border on all sides.

5. Dust the work surface again with flour and roll the second sheet of puff pastry into a slightly larger, 14 x 19-inch rectangle.

6. Whisk the egg with the remaining 2 tablespoons water in a small bowl until smooth. Paint the border of the pastry in the sheet pan with some of this egg wash. Transfer the second sheet of pastry to the sheet pan, making a "crust" over the filling.

7. Seal the edges together all around the pan by pinching them together, folding them over, and scoring them with the tines of a flatware fork. Brush this top sheet of pastry with the remaining egg mixture. Using a sharp knife, make four equidistant slits across the top crust.

8. Bake until the pastry is puffed and golden brown, about 25 minutes. Cool in the pan on a wire rack for at least 20 minutes; serve warm.

TESTER NOTES
You don't need to use all the egg wash. Just get a good coating across the top sheet.

RICE PUDDING PIE

If you love rice pudding, you've come to the right place! This one's sort of a cross between a pie and a pudding: a crust below but the softer, more luxurious texture of a pudding above. You have to chill the whole thing down to cut it into slices. Even so, the portions won't stay perfect at their edges on the plate. We wouldn't fault you if you garnished each serving with a little chocolate sauce.

4 cups water

1 cup raw Arborio or other medium-grain white rice

Single-crust version of All-Butter Crust (page 147)

3 cups whole milk

1 large egg plus 5 large egg yolks, at room temperature

⅔ cup granulated white sugar

2 tablespoons Galliano

¼ cup all-purpose flour

2 tablespoons cornstarch

3 tablespoons unsalted butter, cut into small bits

1 pound whole-milk ricotta

1 tablespoon vanilla extract

2 teaspoons anise seeds

½ teaspoon salt

1 teaspoon ground cinnamon

½ teaspoon freshly grated nutmeg

1. Position the rack in the center of the oven. Heat the oven to 350°F.

2. Bring the water and rice to a boil in a large saucepan set over high heat. Reduce the heat to low and simmer for 15 minutes, stirring occasionally at first, then more and more frequently. Continue cooking, stirring constantly, until the rice is tender, the water has been absorbed, and the mixture looks like thick risotto, about 5 more minutes. Pour into a medium bowl and cool for 20 minutes.

3. Meanwhile, prepare and shape the crust as directed in a 13 x 18-inch lipped sheet pan. Prick the crust repeatedly with a flatware fork, then line the pan with aluminum foil. Bake for 10 minutes, just until partially set. Uncover and set aside on a wire rack while you make the pudding.

4. Whisk 2 tablespoons of the milk, the egg yolks, sugar, and Galliano in a large bowl until smooth. Whisk in the flour and cornstarch until thick and uniform.

5. Bring the remaining 2¾ cups plus 2 tablespoons milk to a very low simmer in a large saucepan set over medium heat. Whisk the hot milk into the egg yolk mixture in a thin, steady stream until uniform. Whisk in the butter until smooth. Cool for 20 minutes.

6. Whisk in the cooked rice as well as the ricotta, whole egg, vanilla, anise seeds, and salt. Pour this mixture into the prepared crust, smoothing it evenly to the sides with an offset spatula. Sprinkle the cinnamon and nutmeg over the top.

7. Bake until lightly browned and a little puffed at the center, and until the custard jiggles slightly at the center of the pan when the rim is tapped, about 30 minutes. Cool in the pan on a wire rack for at least 1 hour before slicing into squares to serve.

TESTER NOTES

We add a little Galliano to the mix for that anise flavor so favored in Italian versions of rice pudding and rice ice cream. You can, of course, omit it without any other additions.

MIDWESTERN SLAB PUDDING

Ages ago, church cookbooks in the Midwest featured a potluck-worthy dessert called a "slab pudding," something like a clafouti, a custard baked over stone fruit, but with more flour for a decidedly more cake-like texture. We hope to bring back this fantastic, potluck-appropriate dessert. But we don't recommend sour cherries for it. They offer too bright a pop, not really in keeping with this down-home treat.

Unsalted butter for the sheet pan
5 large eggs, at room temperature
1¼ cups whole milk
1¼ cups full-fat sour cream
½ cup granulated white sugar
⅓ cup packed light brown sugar
2 teaspoons vanilla extract
½ teaspoon almond extract
1¼ cups all-purpose flour
½ teaspoon baking powder
½ teaspoon salt
3 pounds frozen pitted sweet cherries (do not thaw)

1. Position the rack in the center of the oven. Heat the oven to 350°F. Generously butter the inside of a 13 x 18-inch lipped sheet pan.

2. Whisk the eggs, milk, sour cream, both sugars, vanilla, and almond extract in a large bowl until smooth. Whisk in the flour, baking powder, and salt until uniform. Pour into the prepared sheet pan.

3. Scatter the cherries over the top of the batter. Gently press them down with the side of a silicone spatula, filling the pan almost completely.

4. Bake until puffed and set with no jiggle when the pan is tapped, about 35 minutes. Cool in the pan on a wire rack for at least 45 minutes before serving warm.

TESTER NOTES

The slab pudding will pull back from the sides of the sheet pan as it cools, giving it more of a sponge-cake texture.

NEW ENGLAND CRANBERRY PIE

Here's another retro dessert, sometimes called a pie even though there's no crust. It's never made in a sheet pan, usually in a pie plate, but we couldn't resist adapting it here because we so love its great texture—a cross between a cake and a pie, with a crackly top and a soft, cakey inside. We make this all year round because we stock up on cranberries when they're in season in the fall, carefully squirreling them away in the freezer.

20 tablespoons (2½ sticks) unsalted butter, melted and cooled to room temperature, plus additional for the sheet pan
2½ cups all-purpose flour
2½ cups granulated white sugar
1 teaspoon baking powder
½ teaspoon salt
5 large eggs, at room temperature
2 teaspoons vanilla extract
1½ pounds frozen cranberries (about 5 cups)
1½ cups chopped walnuts

1. Position the rack in the center of the oven. Heat the oven to 350°F. Generously butter the inside of a 13 x 18-inch lipped sheet pan.

2. Whisk the flour, sugar, baking powder, and salt in a large bowl until uniform.

3. Whisk the melted butter, eggs, and vanilla in a second bowl until smooth. Pour into the flour mixture and use a wooden spoon to stir into a very thick batter.

4. Stir in the cranberries and walnuts until uniform. Using an offset spatula, spread the mixture evenly into the prepared pan.

5. Bake until lightly browned and set and a toothpick or cake tester inserted into the center of the cake without touching a cranberry comes out clean, 30 to 35 minutes. Cool in the pan on a wire rack to room temperature, at least 1½ hours, before serving.

TESTER NOTES

We use frozen cranberries so they better retain their shape as they bake. However, once they're added to the batter, it will become super thick, almost paste-like. You'll need to work with a sturdy wooden spoon to get them incorporated—and you'll need to work hard to get the batter spread into the pan. Don't dump it all in the middle. Instead, dollop it all over the pan, then start spreading the pieces together.

ALMOND-HAZELNUT DACQUOISE WITH CHOCOLATE FRENCH BUTTERCREAM

A dacquoise is a meringue cake layer, usually a mix of beaten egg whites and ground nuts. Here (of course), it's turned into something like a Parisian pastry chef's version of a sheet cake. Before you get started, please note that the dacquoise layer requires three hours in the oven, then at least 1½ hours to cool completely at room temperature. Afterwards, you'll top it with a true French buttercream, a frosting made from egg yolks and butter, a true bit of dessert decadence fit for any occasion.

For the dacquoise

Unsalted butter for the parchment paper
3 cups confectioners' sugar
2 cups finely ground toasted skinned hazelnuts
2 cups finely ground almonds
12 large egg whites, at room temperature
¾ cup granulated white sugar

1. Position the rack in the center of the oven and heat the oven to 250°F. Butter a 13 x 18-inch lipped sheet pan, line it with parchment paper, then generously butter the paper and the inside lip of the pan. Stir the confectioners' sugar and both ground nuts in a large bowl until uniform.

2. Using a handheld electric mixer or a stand mixer with the whisk attachment, beat the egg whites in a second large bowl at low speed until foamy, then increase the speed to high and beat until you can form soft peaks, 3 to 4 minutes.

3. Add the white sugar 2 tablespoons at a time, beating at high speed all the while, until thick

and glossy. Scrape down and remove the beaters or whisk. Using a silicone spatula, gently fold in the nut mixture just until uniform throughout without deflating the egg whites. Spread the mixture over the parchment paper in the sheet pan, a moderately thin layer lip to lip.

4. Bake until firm to the touch without browning, about 3 hours. Cool in the pan on a wire rack to room temperature, about 1½ hours. (Do not even start the frosting until the cake layer is at room temperature.)

For the buttercream

6 large egg yolks, at room temperature
¾ cup granulated white sugar
½ cup dark corn syrup
32 tablespoons (4 sticks) unsalted butter, softened to room temperature
8 ounces dark chocolate, preferably 70% cocoa solids, chopped, melted and cooled to room temperature

1. Using a handheld electric mixer or a stand mixer with a whisk attachment, beat the egg yolks in a large bowl at medium speed until light and thick, about 3 minutes. Set aside.

2. Combine the sugar and corn syrup in a medium saucepan. Set it over medium heat and cook, stirring occasionally, until the sugar dissolves. Bring to a boil undisturbed; boil for 1 minute.

3. Beating all the while at medium speed, drizzle this sugar mixture into the egg yolks.

Continue beating at medium speed until the mixture is *fully* room temperature, 10 to 15 minutes. Test it by cupping your palms around the outside of the bowl *and* by turning off the beaters to stick a clean finger right down into the mixture in several places.

4. Beat in the softened butter in 2-tablespoon increments, working slowly but steadily and efficiently. Beat in the chocolate until uniform. Spread and smooth the buttercream over the cooled dacquoise. Serve at once or cover lightly with plastic wrap and store in the refrigerator for up to 1 day.

TESTER NOTES
Look for skinned and roasted hazelnuts at most large supermarkets. Some large markets even carry ground hazelnuts.

COCONUT SHORTBREAD WITH COCONUT LIME CURD

A true curiosity, this one's something like a sweet-sour lime pie, although it's really, of course, a curd poured over shortbread and then cooled. Pay attention to the two types of coconut here, both sweetened and unsweetened. It's important to differentiate them to keep the dessert from becoming too sweet. Of course, you could omit the curd, bake the big slab of shortbread, and top it with the ganache from the No-Bake Cherry-Chocolate Cheesecake (page 107).

For the shortbread
27 tablespoons (3 sticks plus 3 tablespoons) cold unsalted butter, cut into small chunks, plus additional for the sheet pan
3¾ cups all-purpose flour
2 cups sweetened shredded coconut
1 cup confectioners' sugar
¾ cup granulated white sugar
1½ teaspoons baking soda
½ teaspoon salt

1. Position the rack in the center of the oven. Heat the oven to 350°F. Generously butter the inside of a 13 x 18-inch lipped sheet pan.

2. Put the butter, flour, sweetened coconut, both sugars, the baking soda, and salt in a large food processor. Cover and process until finely ground. Pour into the prepared sheet pan. Use clean, dry fingers to press it into an even crust across the bottom of the pan.

3. Bake until light brown and set, about 25 minutes. Transfer to a wire rack to cool while you make the curd.

For the curd

2 cups granulated white sugar

1 cup unsweetened shredded coconut

12 tablespoons (1½ sticks) unsalted butter, cut into small pieces

3 large eggs plus 3 large egg yolks, at room temperature

⅔ cup fresh lime juice

¼ cup coconut cream

1. Put the sugar, unsweetened coconut, butter, eggs, egg yolks, lime juice, and coconut cream in a large saucepan. Set it over low heat and cook, whisking often, until the butter melts. Then cook, whisking constantly, until bubbling and thickened, about 7 minutes.

2. Pour and spread evenly over the shortbread while it's still warm. Cool in the pan on a wire rack for 30 minutes, then refrigerate until set, at least 2 hours or overnight, covering loosely with plastic wrap once chilled.

For the topping

2 cups unsweetened shredded coconut

1. Position the rack in the top third of the oven; heat the oven to 350°F.

2. Spread the unsweetened coconut on a lipped sheet pan. Toast in the oven until lightly browned, stirring occasionally, about 7 minutes. Transfer to a wire rack and cool to room temperature, about 1 hour. Sprinkle evenly over the top of the chilled, set curd.

TESTER NOTES

Coconut cream—*not* cream of coconut, a concoction for tiki drinks—is thick coconut milk found mostly at Asian markets. If you can't find coconut cream, set two cans of full-fat coconut milk in the fridge overnight, then scrape the solid coconut bits off the tops as a substitute.

CHERRY-ALMOND DANISH

You'll need a few tubes of almond paste to make this classic Danish that's been morphed into a slab. Look for tubes that are still soft, not hard and dried out. If possible, avoid marzipan, which can have almond oil in the mix and turn this filling rather boggy. The oven temperature here is a little lower than on the following slab Danish so the filling has a little longer to meld as it bakes.

10 ounces dried cherries (about 1½ cups)
½ cup unsweetened apple or cherry juice
½ cup brandy
2 large eggs, separated, plus 2 large egg whites, at room temperature
1 pound almond paste
1 cup unsweetened shredded coconut
6 tablespoons granulated white sugar
8 tablespoons (1 stick) unsalted butter, softened to room temperature
All-purpose flour, for dusting
One 17.3-ounce box frozen puff pastry (2 sheets), thawed
3 tablespoons water, plus additional as needed

1. Position the rack in the center of the oven. Heat the oven to 375°F.

2. Combine the dried cherries, juice, and brandy in a small saucepan and bring to a simmer over high heat, stirring occasionally. Cover, reduce the heat to low, and simmer slowly for 10 minutes. Cool to room temperature until almost all of the liquid has been absorbed, about 1 hour.

3. Process the egg whites in a food processor until foamy.

4. Add the almond paste and process until smooth. Add the coconut and ¼ cup of the sugar. Again process until smooth. Finally, add the butter, cover, and process until uniform, like a paste.

5. Dust a clean, dry work surface generously with flour. Put one sheet of the puff pastry at the center, dust it with flour, and roll it into a 13 x 18-inch rectangle (for tips, see page 180). Transfer this rectangle to a 13 x 18-inch lipped sheet pan.

6. Spread the almond paste filling evenly over the dough, leaving a ½-inch border on all sides. Sprinkle the cherries evenly over the top.

7. Dust the work surface again with flour. Roll the second piece of puff pastry into a slightly larger, 14 x 19-inch rectangle. Use a small brush or even your clean fingertips to moisten the perimeter of the puff pastry sheet in the pan with water. Set this second sheet on top; press and pinch to seal to the edges all around.

8. Whisk the yolks with 3 tablespoons water in a small bowl. Use a brush to smear this mixture over the top of the second pastry sheet. Sprinkle with the remaining 2 tablespoons sugar. Finally, cut several slits across the top crust, perhaps eight short slits in equidistant spaces down both sides.

9. Bake until puffed and browned, 20 to 25 minutes. Cool in the pan on a wire rack for at least 30 minutes before serving warm.

TESTER NOTES
If you don't want the brandy in the filling, omit it and increase the unsweetened juice to 1 cup.

CHOCOLATE AND GOAT CHEESE DANISH

Imagine a sophisticated mix of chocolate ganache and soft goat cheese. Now imagine it in a Danish. Can't? Then make this treat to see for yourself. Consider it the dessert for some evening when you've got a good bourbon or brandy on hand.

6 ounces dark chocolate, preferably 70% to 80% cocoa solids, chopped
5 ounces soft goat cheese
¾ cup heavy cream
2 tablespoons honey
¼ cup unsweetened cocoa powder
All-purpose flour, for dusting
One 17.3-ounce box frozen puff pastry (2 sheets), thawed
1 large egg
2 tablespoons water

1. Position the rack in the center of the oven. Heat the oven to 400°F.

2. Put the chocolate and goat cheese in a medium bowl. Heat the cream and honey in a small saucepan over medium-low heat, stirring at first to dissolve the honey, until small bubbles fizz around the inside perimeter of the pan. Pour over the chocolate and goat cheese; whisk until smooth. Whisk in the cocoa powder until uniform, then cool for 15 minutes at room temperature.

3. Dust a clean, dry work surface generously with flour. Set one sheet of the pastry in the center, dust it with flour, and roll it into a 13 x 18-inch rectangle, flipping it over once to make sure it's not stuck to the surface. (For more tips, see page 180.) Transfer to a 13 x 18-inch lipped sheet pan.

4. Spread the chocolate mixture evenly across the top in a thin coating, leaving a ½-inch border around all sides. Whisk the egg and water in a small bowl until smooth. Paint the border with this wash.

5. Dust the work surface again with flour and roll out the second sheet of puff pastry into a slightly larger, 13½ x 18½-inch rectangle, using the same technique as in step 3. Transfer it on top of the filling and bottom pastry sheet. Seal the edges closed around the rectangle. Brush the remainder of the egg wash over the top.

6. Bake until puffed and golden brown, and until the pastry has shrunk back a bit from the sheet pan's edges, 20 to 25 minutes. Cool in the pan on a wire rack for at least 30 minutes before serving warm.

TESTER NOTES
You can dramatically alter the flavor of this Danish based on the honey you use. Yes, there are sweet wildflower or clover honeys aplenty in our supermarkets. But search out other types: blueberry, orange blossom, star thistle, chestnut, even dark tree honeys like oak or pine. Just avoid any with artificial (or even "natural") flavors in the mix.

CHEESE DANISH

The filling is fairly simple, really just a sweetened cheese mixture. You can add some flavorings, if you like: anise seeds, grated nutmeg, even decorticated cardamom seeds for a very elegant finish. In any event, consider this Danish an easy way to get started making these big-format treats.

1 pound whole-milk ricotta
8 ounces full-fat cream cheese
½ cup granulated white sugar
1 teaspoon vanilla extract
All-purpose flour, for dusting
One 17.3-ounce box frozen puff pastry (2
    sheets), thawed
1 large egg
2 tablespoons water

1. Position the rack in the center of the oven. Heat the oven to 400°F.

2. Place the ricotta, cream cheese, sugar, and vanilla in a food processor. Cover and process until creamy, about 1 minute.

3. Dust a clean, dry work surface generously with flour. Set one sheet of the pastry in the center, dust it generously with flour, and roll it into a 13 x 18-inch rectangle. Transfer to a 13 x 18-inch lipped sheet pan. (For tips on working with puff pastry, see page 180.)

4. Spread the cheese mixture on top, leaving a ½-inch border around all sides. Whisk the egg and water in a small bowl until smooth. Paint that border with this wash.

5. Dust the work surface again with flour and roll out the second sheet of puff pastry to a slightly larger 13½ x 18½-inch rectangle. Transfer it on top of the filling and first sheet. Seal the edges closed around the rectangle. Brush the remainder of the egg mixture over the top.

6. Bake until puffed and golden brown, about 30 minutes. Cool in the pan on a wire rack for at least 30 minutes before serving warm.

TESTER NOTES
The dough should fill the pan when it's rolled out; however, it will shrink from all sides as it bakes, creating a slightly smaller rectangle inside, perhaps malformed along some browned edges.

ALMOND PHYLLO ROLLS

Here's our slab pie version of baklava. Well, sort of. It's actually a line-up of phyllo rolls, baked together in that by-now-familiar sheet pan, then topped with a hot sugar syrup that will make the phyllo extra crisp. The trick is for the rolls to be quite hot from the oven when you pour the warm syrup over them. If not, they'll turn sticky. Serve them like a cake, cutting across the rolls to form pieces with sections of two or three rolls in each.

One 5-ounce can coconut oil spray
1½ pounds raw whole almonds (about 4½ cups)
1 cup packed dark brown sugar
4½ teaspoons ground cinnamon
½ teaspoon salt
One 1-pound box frozen phyllo sheets, thawed
1 cup granulated white sugar
⅔ cup water
½ cup honey
1 tablespoon molasses
2 teaspoons orange flower water, optional

1. Position the rack in the center of the oven. Heat the oven to 350°F. Generously coat the inside of a 13 x 18-inch lipped sheet pan with coconut oil spray.

2. Pulse the almonds, brown sugar, cinnamon, and salt in a food processor until finely ground. Pour this mixture into a medium bowl.

3. Unwrap the phyllo sheets, lay them on a clean, dry work surface, and cover them with a clean kitchen towel. Lay one sheet of phyllo dough on a clean, dry work surface; lightly coat the sheet with coconut oil spray. Turn it over and coat the other side. Lay a second sheet on top and spray it with coconut oil. Sprinkle ¼

cup of the nut mixture over the surface. Roll the two sheets up like a cigar from the short end. Place it in the prepared sheet pan at a corner and along one long edge; spray it lightly with the coconut oil. (It will reach about halfway down the length of the pan.)

4. Now prepare a second cigar just as the first and place it end to end with the first one. Then continue making more cigars, creating 20 in all, using them to fill the pan. You'll need to scrunch them a bit to get to them to fit.

5. Spray the top of the whole sheet pan of rolls generously with coconut oil. Then bake until golden brown and crisp, about 25 minutes.

6. Meanwhile, mix the sugar, water, honey, molasses, and orange flower water, if using, in a small saucepan. Stir over medium heat until the sugar and honey dissolve. Bring to a simmer, then reduce the heat and simmer slowly for 2 minutes undisturbed. Cover, remove from the heat, and set aside to keep warm.

7. Transfer the hot sheet pan to a wire rack. Pour the warm syrup over the hot rolls. Cool in the pan to room temperature, for at least 1½ hours, before serving.

SPICED PISTACHIO PHYLLO CAKE

Here's another "sort of" baklava dessert. This one's a cross between the classic and a sheet cake. Or perhaps it's a sheet cake made with phyllo dough, then scored into serving-size portions before being baked. All in all, it's a flaky curiosity that's served with a rosewater-scented whipped cream to make an elegant dessert after a tagine, a curry, or almost anything off the grill.

One 5-ounce can coconut oil spray
4 cups unsalted shelled pistachios
1 cup granulated white sugar
1 teaspoon ground cinnamon
½ teaspoon ground cardamom
½ teaspoon ground cloves
One 1-pound box frozen phyllo sheets, thawed
2 cups heavy cream
¼ cup confectioners' sugar
1 teaspoon rosewater

1. Position the rack in the center of the oven. Heat the oven to 350°F. Generously coat the inside of a 13 x 18-inch lipped sheet pan with coconut oil spray.

2. Pulse the pistachios, sugar, cinnamon, cardamom, and cloves in a food processor until finely ground. Pour into a small bowl.

3. Unwrap the phyllo sheets, lay them on a clean, dry work surface, and cover them with a clean kitchen towel. Place one or two sheets of phyllo in the prepared pan (depending on their size, for coverage). Spray the sheet with coconut oil. Sprinkle about ¼ cup of the pistachio mixture evenly over the sheets.

4. Repeat with another sheet or two, more spray, and another ¼ cup pistachio mixture, creating a second layer. Then keep going, making more layers just like this, until you run out of the nut mixture. Top with two more sheets of phyllo and coat well with the coconut oil spray.

5. Using a paring knife, cut the sheets into 24 rectangles—that is, making three equidistant cuts the long way and 5 equidistant cuts the short way.

6. Bake until golden brown and crisp, about 25 minutes. Cool in the pan on a wire rack for at least 1 hour.

7. Using a handheld electric mixer or a stand mixer with the whisk attachment, beat the cream in a large bowl at high speed until you can make soft peaks. Beat in the confectioners' sugar and rosewater. Serve the rectangles topped with this scented whipped cream.

TESTER NOTES
If you can only find salted pistachios, rinse them repeatedly with cool water in a colander, tossing them to rearrange them as the water runs over them. Dry thoroughly between lots of paper towels. The dessert will still be saltier but perhaps that's not a bad thing in your book.

GALAKTOBOUREKO

This traditional Greek dessert is a semolina-thickened custard that's layered between lots of phyllo sheets. Unlike a napoleon, that French favorite, the creamy custard is here baked with the phyllo, not added later. We use more phyllo than many more standard recipes because we love crunch. (Did we mention that enough? If something doesn't shard, is it really worth eating?) No doubt about it, this one's a crazy way to end the book, a real crowd-pleaser.

20 tablespoons (2½ sticks) unsalted butter, melted and cooled to room temperature, plus additional as needed and for the sheet pan
2½ cups plus 2 tablespoons granulated white sugar
¾ cup water
4 wide strips orange zest sliced into matchsticks, plus 6 tablespoons fresh orange juice
4 wide strips lemon zest, sliced into matchsticks
6 tablespoons honey
2 teaspoons orange flower water
4½ cups whole milk
9 tablespoons semolina flour
4 large eggs plus 1 large egg yolk, at room temperature
1 tablespoon vanilla extract
½ teaspoon salt
One 1-pound box frozen phyllo sheets, thawed

1. Position the rack in the center of the oven. Heat the oven to 350°F. Generously butter the inside of a 13 x 18-inch lipped sheet pan.

2. Mix 1½ cups of the sugar, the water, orange zest, orange juice, lemon zest, honey, and orange flower water in a medium saucepan. Stir over medium heat until the sugar dissolves, then bring to a simmer. Reduce the heat to low and simmer undisturbed for 7 minutes. Set aside off the heat while you prepare the pastry.

3. Bring the milk to a low simmer in a large saucepan set over medium heat. Reduce the heat to low and whisk in the semolina flour until thick and porridge-like, 12 to 15 minutes. Cool for 10 minutes.

4. Meanwhile, using a handheld electric mixer or a stand mixer with the whisk attachment, beat the remaining 1 cup plus 2 tablespoons sugar, eggs, and egg yolk in a large bowl at medium speed until you can make wide ribbons, about 5 minutes.

5. Beating at medium speed all the while, pour in the hot semolina mixture in a slow, steady stream, then beat in the vanilla and salt until smooth.

6. Unwrap the phyllo sheets, lay them on a clean, dry work surface, and cover them with a clean kitchen towel. Depending on what size phyllo you're working with, place one large or two more standard sheets in the bottom of the prepared sheet pan to make an even layer, then brush with the melted butter. Continue making layers in the pan until you've used about two-thirds of the phyllo sheets.

7. Pour and spread the semolina mixture evenly over the phyllo sheets. Then continue building up more layers with more sheets and more melted butter until you've used them all to create a many-layered phyllo cake in the pan. Brush the top generously with melted butter, even if you have to melt a little more.

8. Bake until puffed and golden brown, about 30 minutes. Transfer in the pan to a wire rack and let the phyllo cake deflate for about 5 minutes. Meanwhile, warm up the sugar syrup in its saucepan by setting it over medium-high heat just until it's hot, not simmering.

9. Pour the hot syrup over the top of the phyllo cake, getting it evenly distributed with lots of strips of the orange and lemon zest across the top. (Spread these out with a fork if they clump together.) Cool in the pan on the rack to room temperature, about 2 hours, before serving.

ACKNOWLEDGMENTS

Even after twenty-nine books, we can't do it on our own! This one's thanks to . . .

Susan Ginsburg and Stacy Testa at Writer's House;

BJ Berti, Gwen Hawkes, Kristopher Kam, Lisa Davis, Karen Lumley, Erica Martirano, Michelle McMillian, and Young Lim at St. Martin's;

David Venable at QVC for his ongoing support;

Lisa Ton at Dole Packed Foods, LLC, for a generous supply of frozen fruit;

Gretchen Holt and her team at OXO for a stack of 18 x 13-inch sheet pans;

Jenna Llewellyn at Digitas and her always supportive client, KitchenAid, for a new mixer to make all these cakes;

Danielle Dexter at 5WPR and her client Krups for a crazy-good espresso machine;

Grainne Sweetman at Ketchum for boxes and boxes of chocolate from Nestlé;

Tom Payne and Katie Walker at King Arthur Flour for boxes and boxes of flour;

Kathy Blackshaw at Pine Hill Farms for donating more than two hundred eggs;

the members of the literary seminar at the Scoville library in Salisbury, Connecticut, as well as those of the book group at the Norfolk library in Norfolk, Connecticut—they ate enough cake and pie to make up for all the James and Brontë they had to read.

INDEX